AF272991

BOARD N'STONES

FSC
www.fsc.org

Fukui Masaaki

KEEP FIT! WITH THE 5×5 BOARD

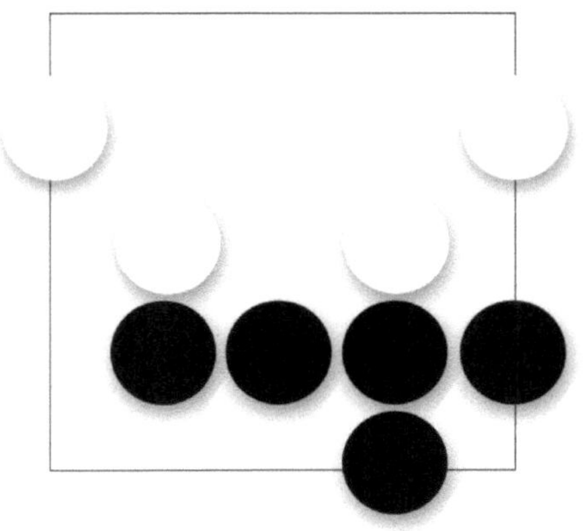

BOARD N'STONES

囲碁特訓 五×五−五道盤上達法
by Fukui Masaaki

Original Japanese edition published by Nihon Kiin.

The German National Library lists this publication in the Deutsche National-bibliografie; detailed bibliographic data are available in the Internet at https://dnb.dnb.de.

Many thanks to Craig for the review of the English translation!

ISBN 978-3-940563-92-7

Translation: Gunnar Dickfeld
Cover design: Lars Decker
Print: Books on Demand GmbH, Norderstedt

The diagrams in this book were created with SmartGo™: http://www.smartgo.com

Preface

Some people may think that the 5×5 board is just a reduced version of Go, but I believe that much of what is complex and profound in Go can still be found in the tight confines of the 5×5 board. So I have been trying a new method of keeping myself fit and improving my Go. The following book was originally published and serialized in "Weekly Go" from January to August of 1998 under the title of "Special Training Room for Higher Speed and Endgame Improvement". I was encouraged to see how well the book was received.

When I started the series, I realized that the 5×5 game was not only about the endgame. Except for the opening, it was about the whole game of Go. It covers partial endgame moves, aspects of life and death, attacking and defending, judgments based on calculating territory, the presence or absence of ko threats, and even things pertaining to the realm of middle game fighting.

This book is primarily for beginners, especially beginners who are just becoming familiar with the endgame, but I have been told that it is also fun for Dan-level players too who may also benefit from this as a good training.

I am proud to say that this book is very useful for improving the understanding of shapes, ko fights, the multiple meanings behind each move and so on. It is said that the number of beginners is increasing dramatically. I hope that this book will help continue to popularize the game of Go.

Midsummer of 2000
Fukui Masaaki

Chapter 1: HOP

Black to play and win!

1

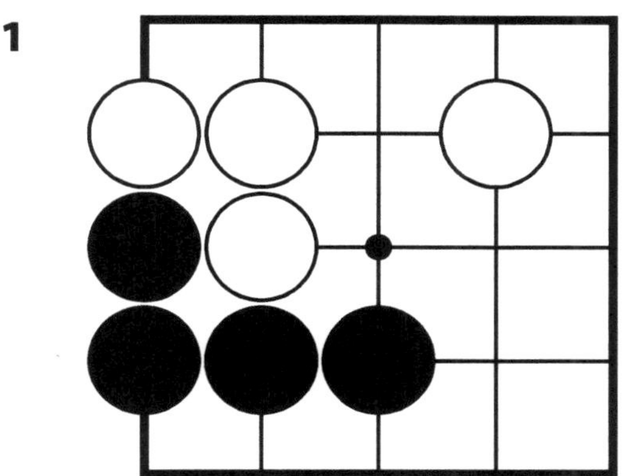

The first move is decisive

2

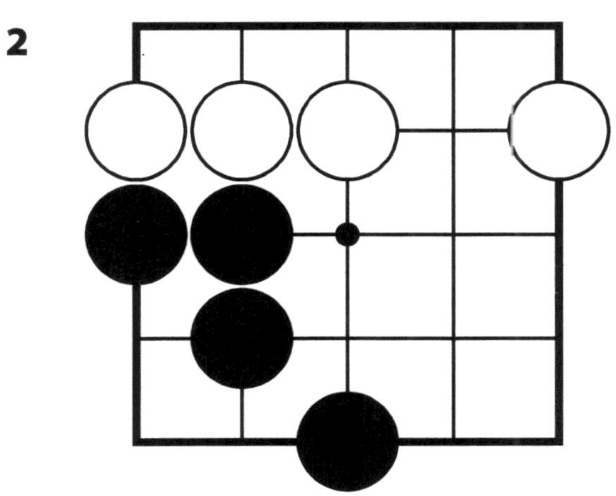

The corner is big

Solution 1 **Black wins by one point.**

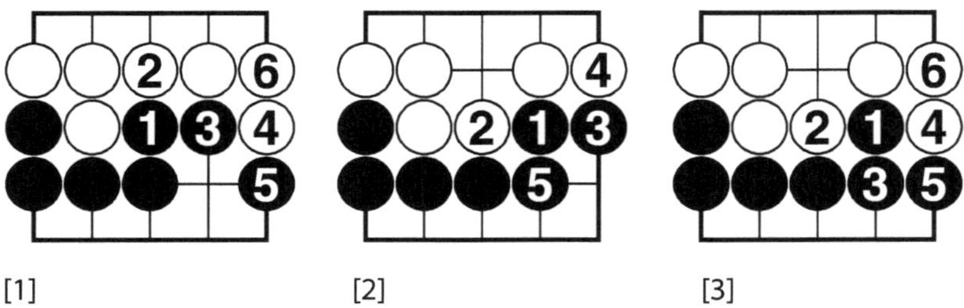

[1] [2] [3]

Dia. 1 (Correct) Black 1 takes the key point. When White answers at 2, Black plays at 3. With White 4 to 6 the game ends. Black has six points and White has five, hence Black wins by one point.

Dia. 2 (Failure) The attachement at 1 allows White to occupy the key point with 2, forcing Black to defend with 3 and to connect at 5 after White plays 4. The result is jigo, Black fails to win.

Dia. 3 (Variation) If Black connects with 3, he is beaten by White 4: Black loses by one point.

Solution 2 **Black wins by one point.**

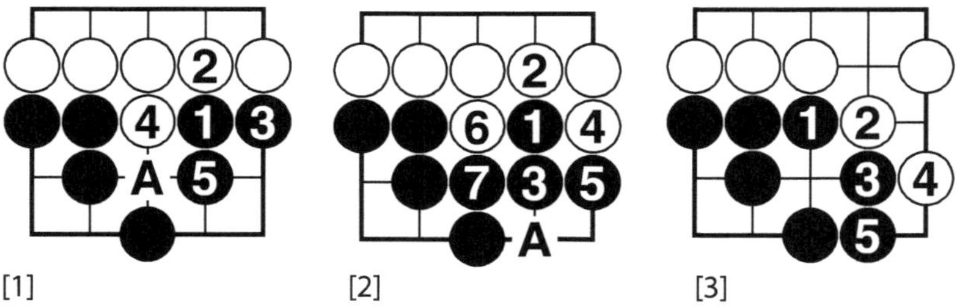

[1] [2] [3]

Dia. 1 (Correct) Black's peep at 1 and the block at 3 are correct. After White 4, Black defends at 5 and wins by one point. In this form, White gets the point A, but Black does not need to worry about it.

Dia. 2 (Failure) It is a mistake to draw back with Black 3. White can take 4 first, and Black 7 is needed. In the end, the result is jigo. If White is allowed to play at 7, Black must add another move at A.

Dia. 3 (Failure) Black 1 is a poor move as White is allowed to play 2 and 4. Black loses by two points.

3

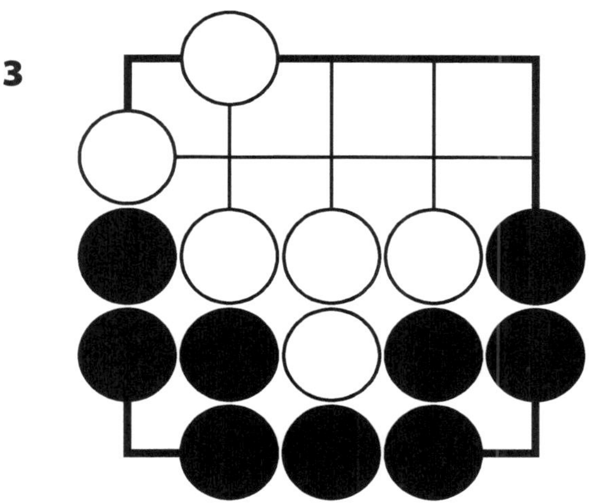

The shortest match

4

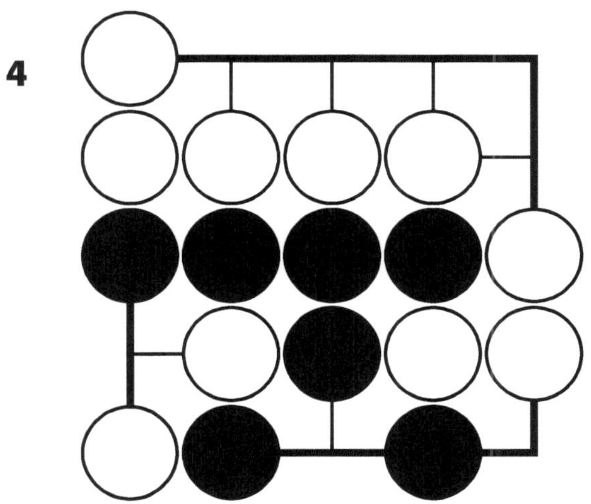

Alive, but…

Solution 3 **Black wins by one point.**

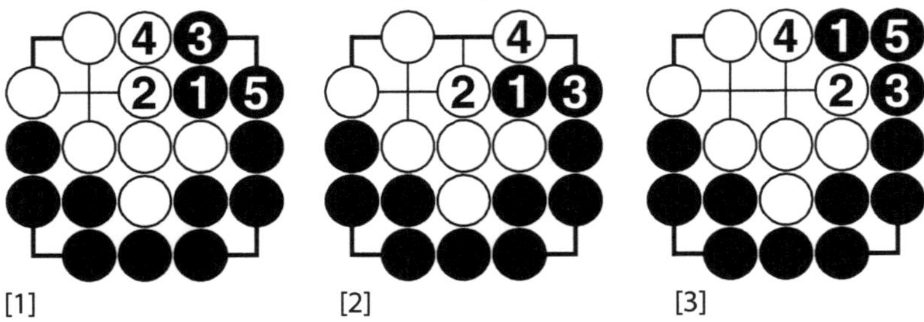

[1] [2] [3]

Dia. 1 (Correct) The correct answer is the hane with Black 1, followed by White 2 and Black's extension at 3. After White 4 and Black 5, Black wins by one point. If White throws in with 4 at 5, the result will be the same because Black gains a captured stone.

Dia. 2 (Failure) Connecting with Black 3 is a mistake. White will play at 4 and the result is jigo. The move at 4 is the key point.

Dia. 3 (Failure) If Black jumps to 1, White will counter at 2 and Black loses by one point.

Solution 4 **Black wins by one point.**

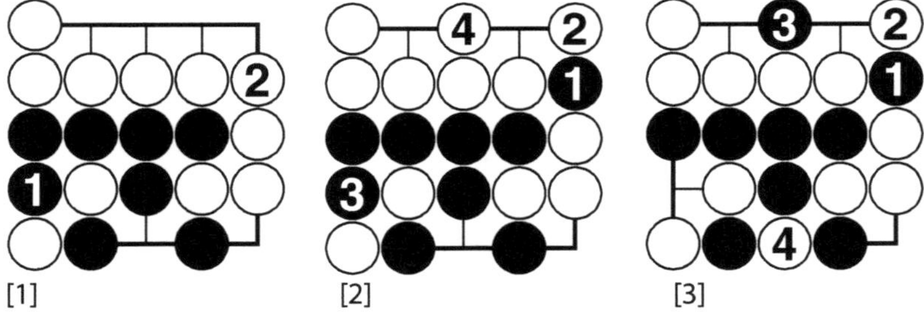

[1] [2] [3]

Dia. 1 (Failure) It looks like the end of the game already. However, it would be a mistake to capture with Black 1 and let White connect at 2. You have to be attentive until the very end.

Dia. 2 (Correct) The first move to play is Black 1. This is the correct way to force White 2 before Black plays 3. Now, White 4 is necessary to make life and Black wins by one point.

Dia. 3 (Variation) Black 1 and 3 would be a failure. White captures a stone at 4 and starts a ko. Black lacks a ko threat and can not win this fight.

5

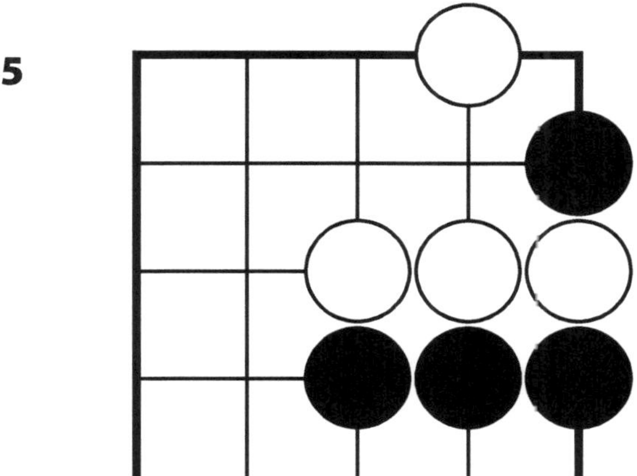

A tesuji worth three points

6

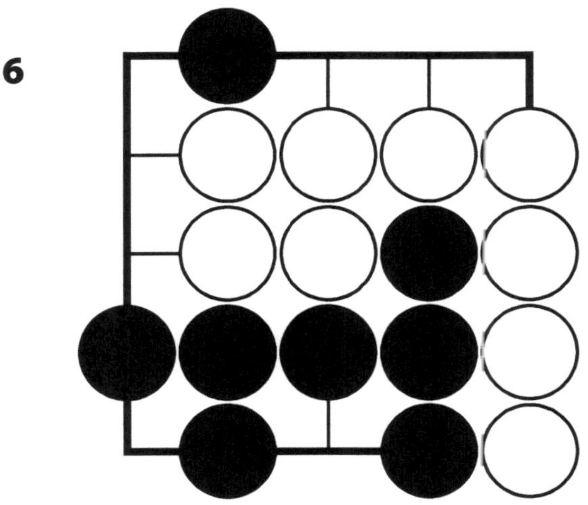

White's weakness

Solution 5 **Black wins by one point.**

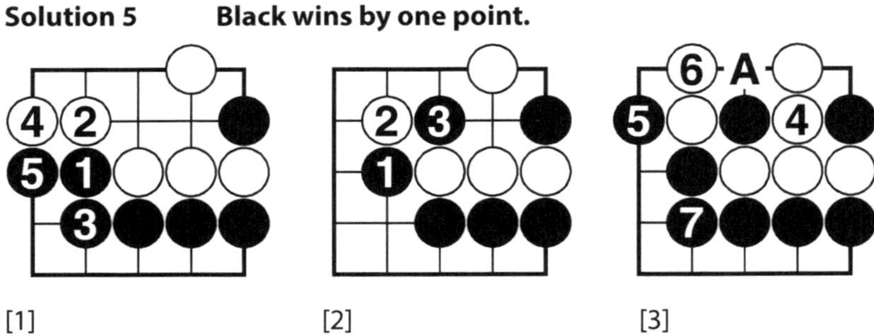

[1] [2] [3]

Dia. 1 (Failure) The moves of Black 1 and 3 are normal ones. After White 4, Black blocks at 5. Black has six points and White has eight. This is clearly a failure.

Dia. 2 (Correct) The best way to play here is the cut at 3.

Dia. 3 (Continuation) When White answers at 4, Black can play atari at 5. Later, White needs to defend at A. The game ends with Black 7. Black wins by one point.

Solution 6 **Black wins by one point.**

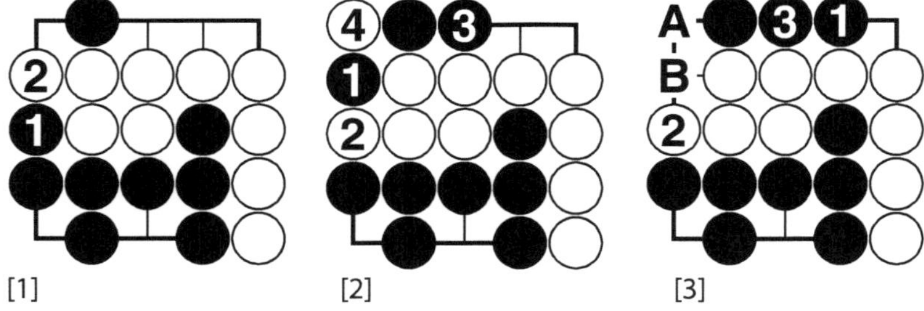

[1] [2] [3]

Dia. 1 (Failure) If the game ends with the mediocre moves Black 1 and White 2, Black will lose by four points.

Dia. 2 (Failure) Black 1 aims at a ko, but that is also a failure because Black has no ko threat when White counters with 2 and 4. White must not play 2 at 3, because Black will kill at 2.

Dia. 3 (Correct) Black 1 is the crucial point. If White blocks at 2 Black will connect at 3. Black wins by two points. White cannot play at A as there is no ko threat to play the ko after Black captures at B. Even if White plays 2 at B, Black wins by making a seki with 3.

7

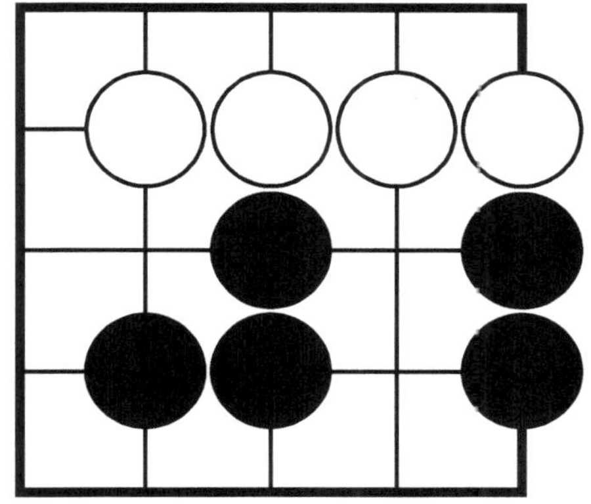

A one point endgame, but…

8

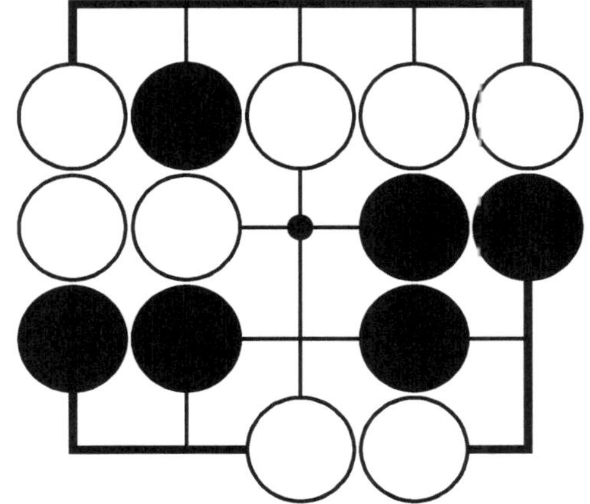

A ko in the corner…

Solution 7 **Black wins by one point.**

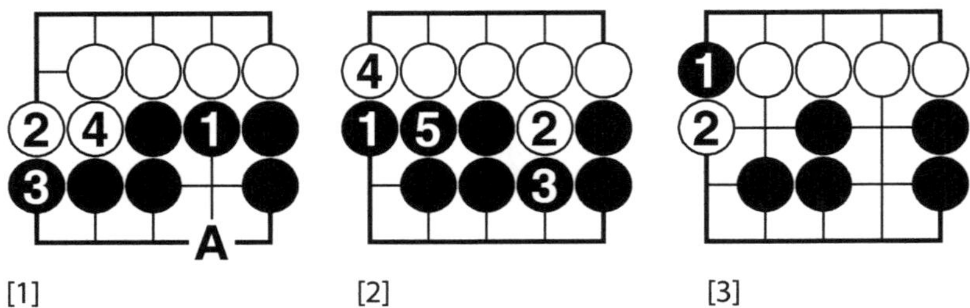

[1] [2] [3]

Dia. 1 (Failure) After Black 1, White will prevent Black's push along the side. The game ends with Black blocking at 3 and White 4. Both sides have six points. Jigo is a failure for Black. If Black plays 3 at 4, White will push at 3 and Black must then defend at A.

Dia. 2 (Correct) It is correct to play at Black 1 first. This is the crucial point. After Black 3 and 5, Black wins by one point.

Dia. 3 (Failure) Black cannot jump to 1. White will counter with 2 and Black cannot gain sufficient points to win.

Solution 8 **Black wins by one point.**

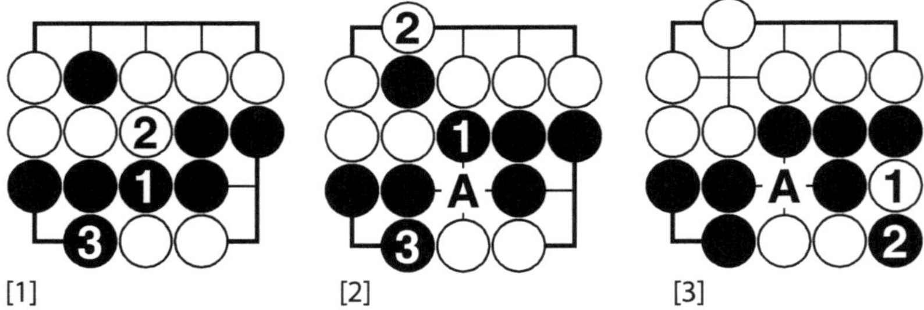

[1] [2] [3]

Dia. 1 (Failure) Black 1 is a mistake. If Black omits 3, White can play there to create a seki. The result is jigo.

Dia. 2 (Correct) It is correct to play Black 1 and then defend at 3. If White gets to play at 3, there will be a seki again.

Dia. 3 (Continuation) Next, if White plays at 1 to start a ko, Black takes the ko first. White passes, as no ko threats are available, and Black finishes the ko at A. This way Black wins by one point.

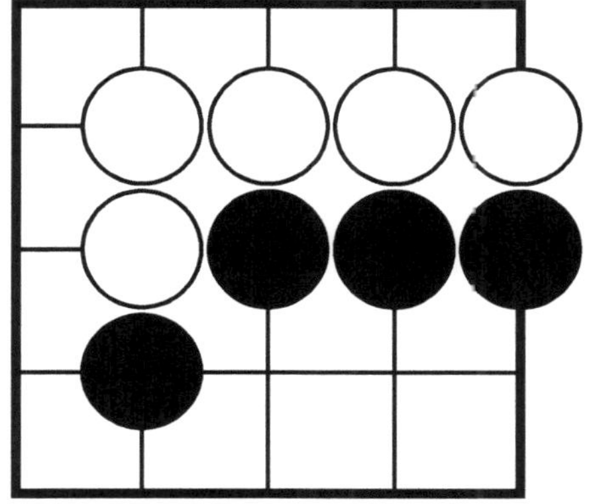

Keep calm

10

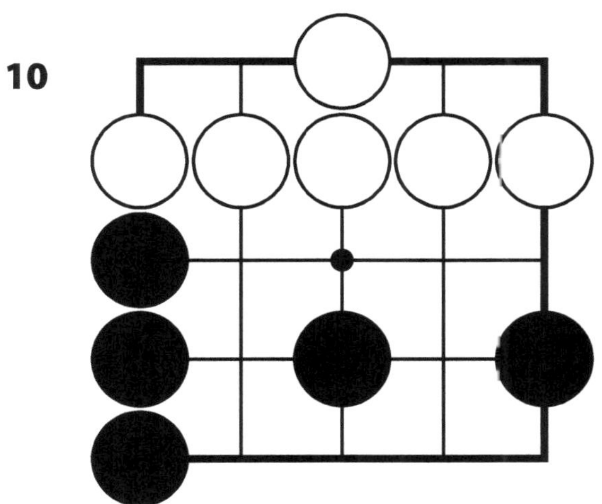

There shall be five points

Solution 9 Black wins by one point.

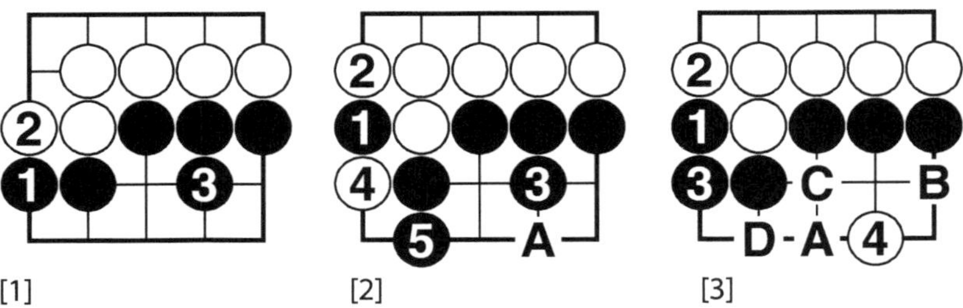

[1] [2] [3]

Dia. 1 (Correct) Black 1 is the correct answer. After White blocks at 2, the game ends with Black 3. There are seven points for Black and six for White. Black wins by one point.

Dia. 2 (Failure) Being greedy is a mistake. After White 2, Black must defend at 3. White 4 and Black 5 follow, but still there is another move needed to remove the aji of White A. Black loses by two points.

Dia. 3 (Failure) If Black connects at 3, White will attack at 4. When Black defends at A, White B threatens a snapback. After Black C and White D, Black's territory has turned into zero points. It is a seki.

Solution 10 Black wins by one point.

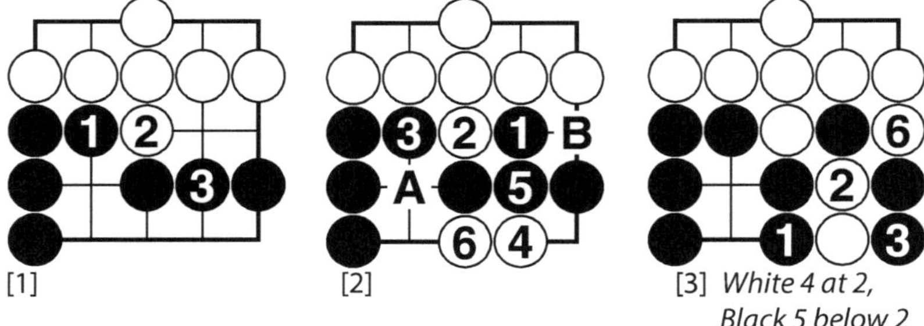

[1] [2] [3] *White 4 at 2, Black 5 below 2*

Dia. 1 (Correct) Black 1 is the crucial point. The game ends with White 2 and Black 3. Black has five points, White only four. Black wins.

Dia. 2 (Failure) Black 1 fails, and Black dies. With White 2 and Black 3, the same moves as in the previous diagram are played, followed by White 4 to 6. If Black plays 3 at A, White will kill with 4. Also, Black 3 at 4 is answered by White B, Black 5 and White A. If Black plays 1 at 5, then White 3 and Black A lead to jigo.

Dia. 3 (Variation) Instead of 5 in the previous diagram, Black 1 here is no better: Black dies.

11

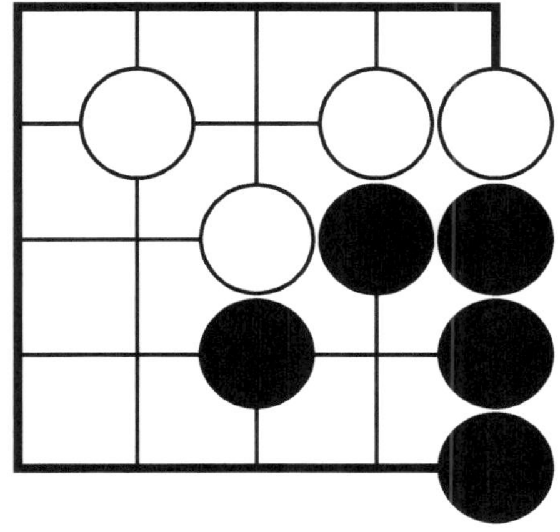

Be careful

12

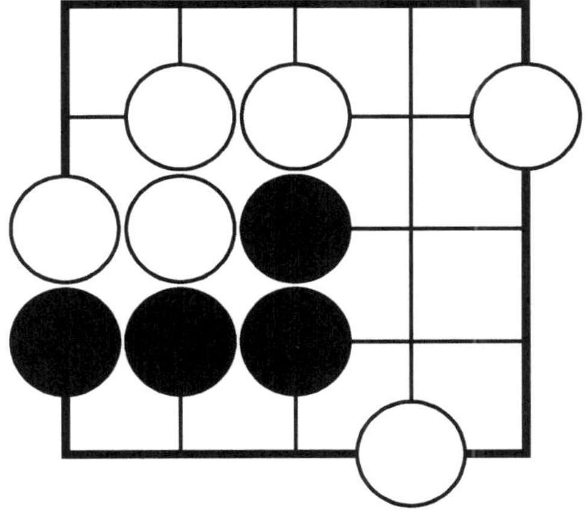

Greed doesn't get you anywhere

Solution 11 Black wins by one point.

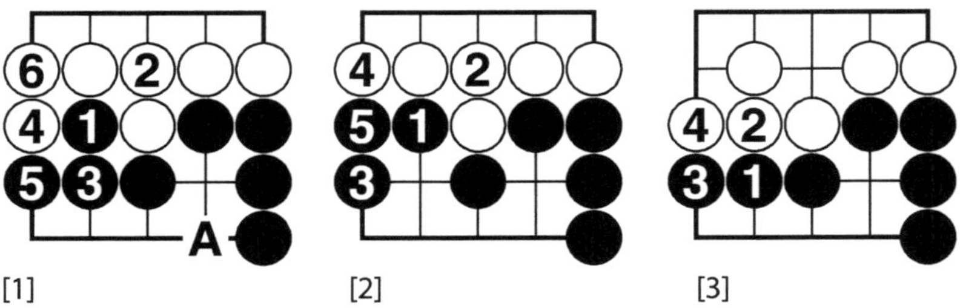

Dia. 1 (Failure) Black 1 is a move to be played, but after White 2 Black's connection at 3 is careless. If Black plays 3 at 4 to extend to the edge, White has the atari at A and then cuts at 3.

Dia. 2 (Correct) Black 1 and connecting at 3 are the way to win in this position. After White 4, Black plays 5 and wins by one point.

Dia. 3 (Failure) After extending at 1, White plays 2 and 4 and Black loses by two points.

Solution 12 Black wins by one point.

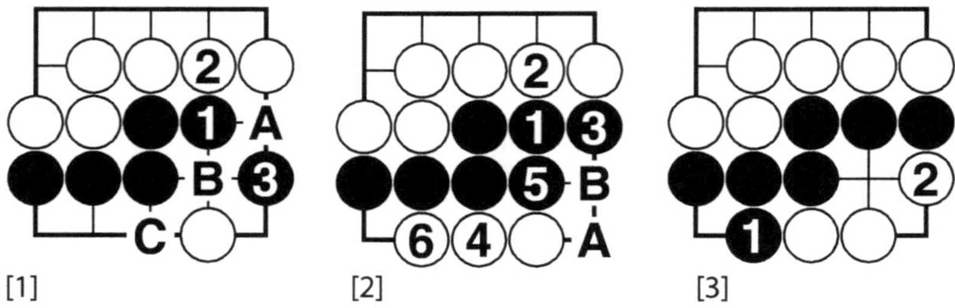

Dia. 1 (Correct) Black 1 takes the crucial point. When White 2 is played, Black 3 is the correct response. Even if White gets A, Black does not need to take further action. The cut with White B is countered by Black C. Black wins by one point.

Dia. 2 (Failure) It is bad to be greedy with Black 1 and 3 here. White will counter with 4 and 6. Next, Black A will be captured by White B. Black lacks a ko threat and loses.

Dia. 3 (Failure) Instead of 5 in the previous diagram, Black 1 allows White to create a seki with 2.

13

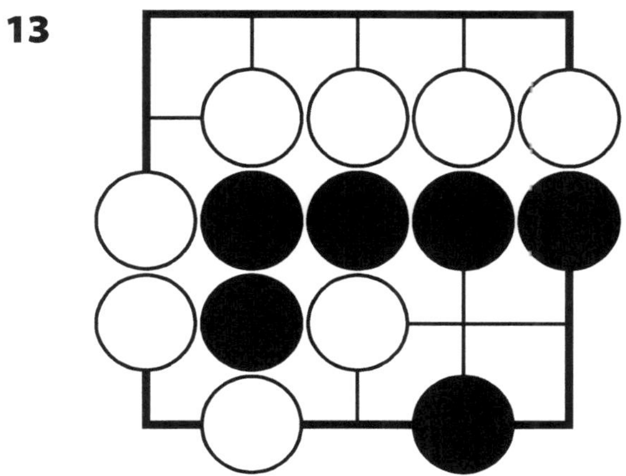

A ko in the corner

14

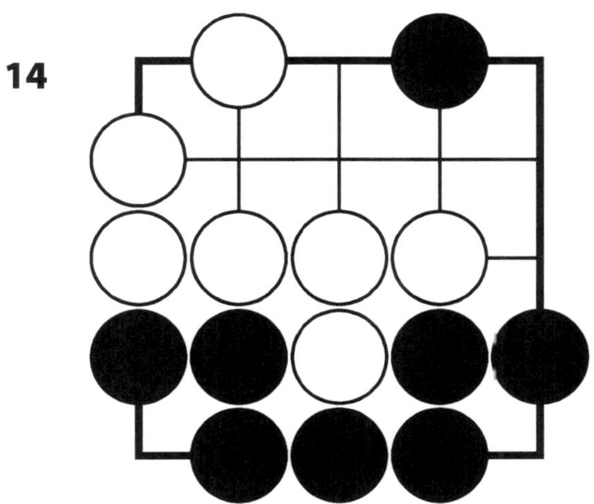

How to get one point more

Solution 13   Black wins by one point.

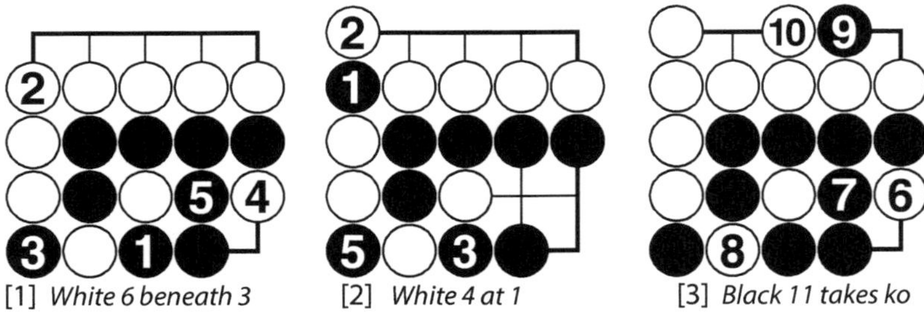

[1] *White 6 beneath 3*   [2] *White 4 at 1*   [3] *Black 11 takes ko*

Dia. 1 (Failure) Cutting with Black 1 is a mistake. Black takes the ko with 3, and that's it. When White plays 4 as a ko threat, Black 5 is forced, and White 6 retakes the ko. Black has no ko threat, so the result is jigo.

Dia. 2 (Correct) Black 1 is a good sacrifice move in order to create a ko threat.

Dia. 3 (Continuation) After the same sequence as in diagram 1, Black now has 9 as a ko threat. Black can take the ko with 11, and thus wins by one point.

Solution 14   Black wins by one point.

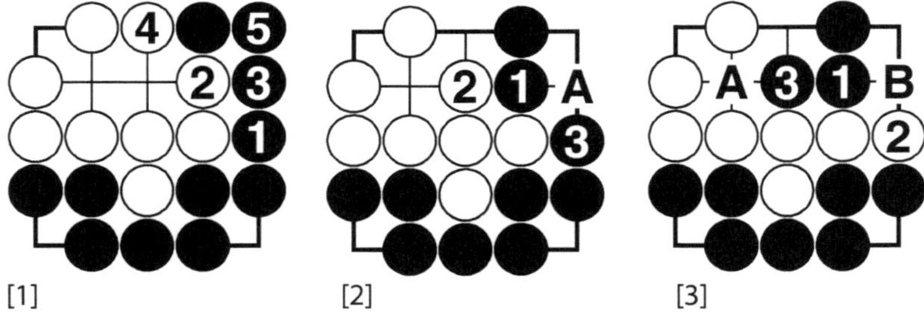

[1]   [2]   [3]

Dia. 1 (Failure) Simply playing Black 1 is not enough. White 2 and 4 are common moves. After Black 5, Black has two points and White three.

Dia. 2 (Correct) Black's bump at 1 is crucial. If White defends at 2, Black plays 3 and wins by one point. The upper right corner is another point for Black: Black connects at A, or White sacrifices a stone at A – either way Black has a point.

Dia. 3 (Variation) If White resists with 2 here, Black 3 creates a seki within White's area, thus Black wins by two points. If White A, Black will play B; and vice versa.

15

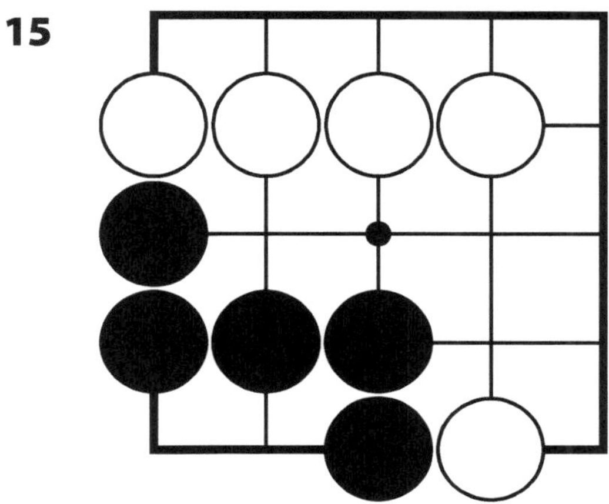

Don't hold back

16

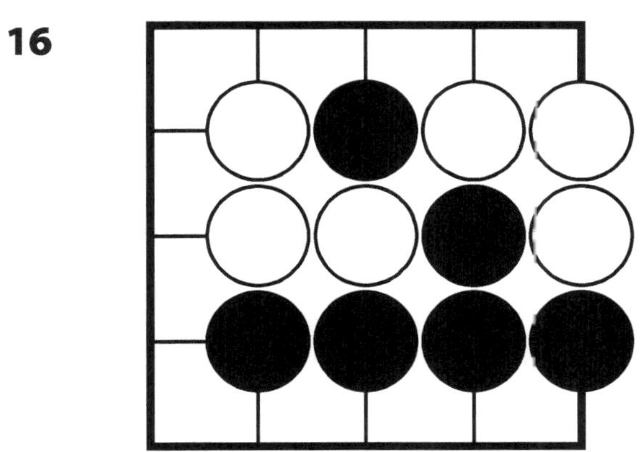

Detect White's defect

Solution 15 Black wins by one point.

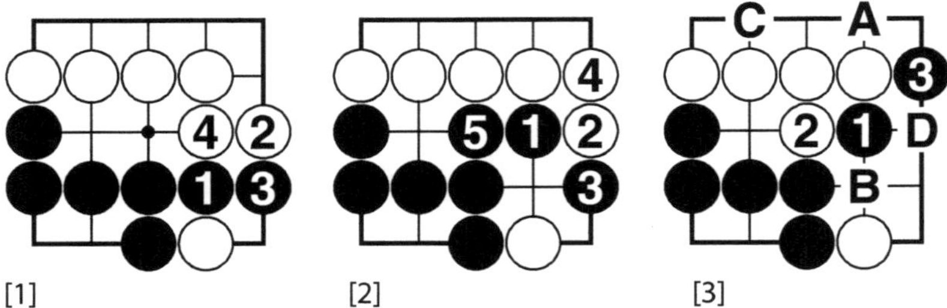

Dia. 1 (Failure) Black's block at 1 is too reserved. Now, White's kosumi at 2 takes the key point. With Black 3 and White 4 the game is finished. Black loses by one point.

Dia. 2 (Correct) Black's attachment at 1 is the correct answer. After the hane and connect with White 2 and 4, Black defends at 5. Black wins by one point.

Dia. 3 (Variation) If White answers at 2, Black's hane is a strong move. White A, Black B, White C, and Black D end the game. If White plays B first, Black simply defends at D.

Solution 16 Black wins by one point.

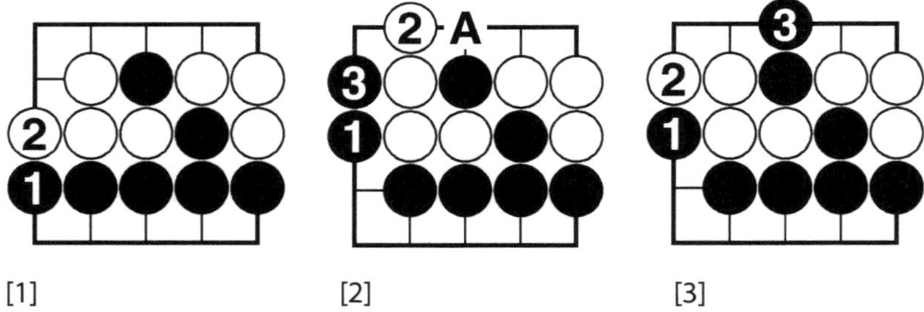

Dia. 1 (Failure) If the game ends with Black extending at 1 and White blocking at 2, Black loses by three points.

Dia. 2 (Correct) Black 1 is correct. White has no choice but to extend to 2 and let Black push further with 3. At the end of the game, White must capture a stone at A. Since Black has 5 points at the bottom, Black wins by one point.

Dia. 3 (Variation) If Black 1 is answered by White 2, Black will extend at 3. White cannot approach the two stones to capture, and thus dies.

17

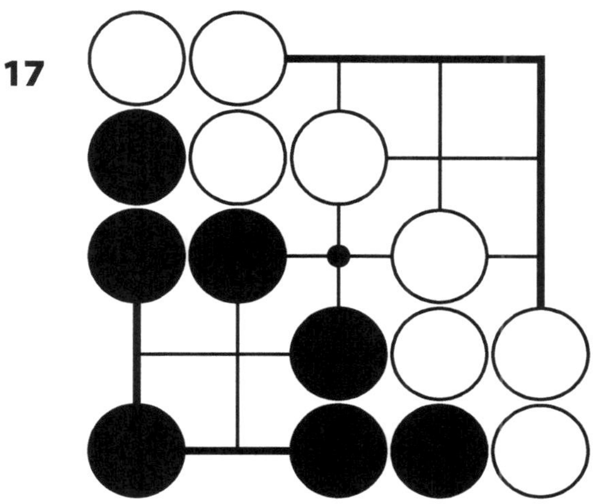

Reverse motion

18

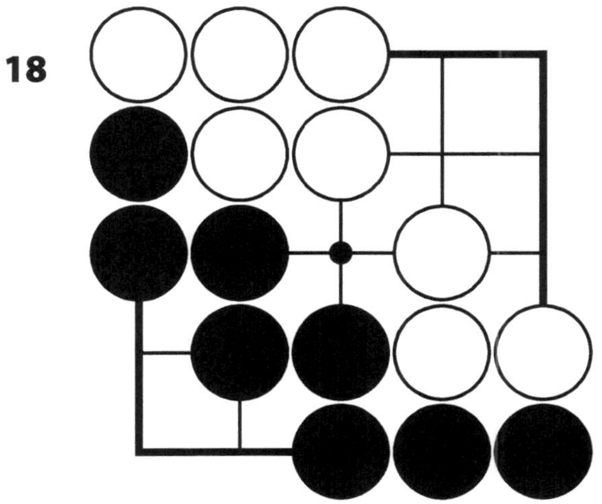

Even if you live with two eyes

Solution 17 Black wins by two points.

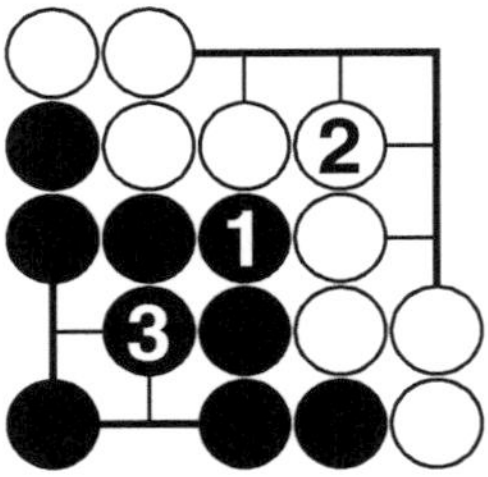

[1] 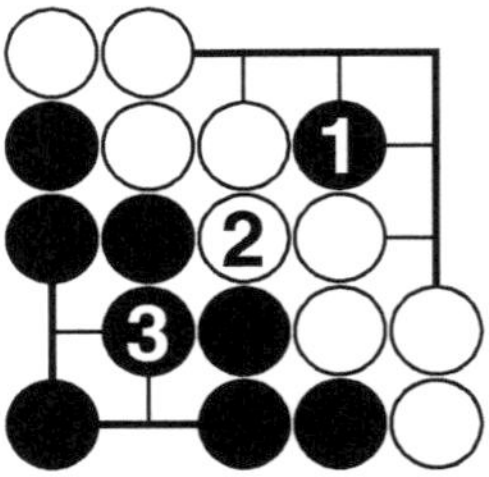 [2] 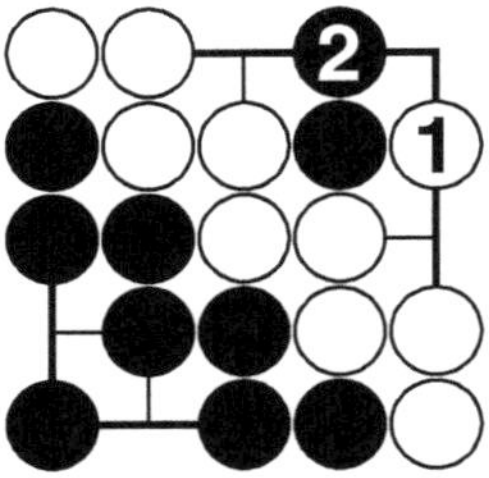 [3]

Dia. 1 (Failure) Black 1 as the first move is bad. After White 2, Black must make life with 3. This is too inept. Black loses by three points.

Dia. 2 (Correct) Black strikes at 1, taking advantage of the special nature of the corner. After White 2, Black again secures life with 3. However, White's corner is now seki. Thus Black wins by two points.

Dia. 3 (Continuation) If White plays atari at 1, Black simply extends at 2.

Solution 18 Black wins.

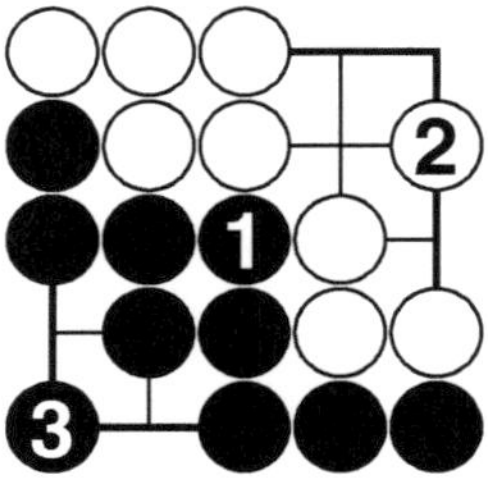

B - A

[1] 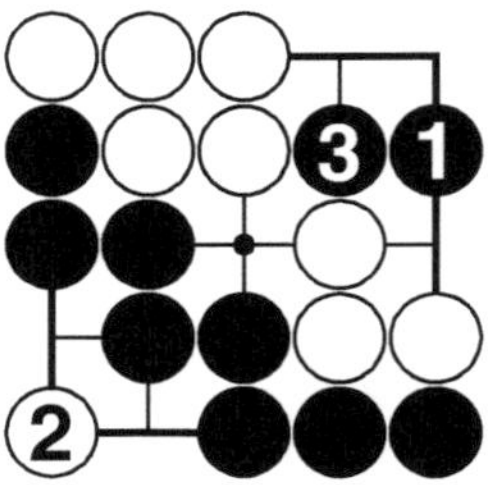 [2] 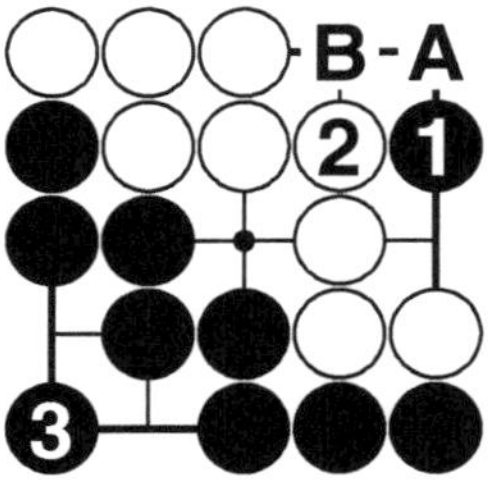 [3]

Dia. 1 (Failure) Neither side has two eyes. If Black plays 1 and 3 to live, he will lose by two points. Even if Black plays 1 at 3, White will simply answer at 2 and win.

Dia. 2 (Correct) The correct answer is to preempt with Black 1. If White strikes back with 2, Black will extend at 3 and win the capturing race. There is no way for White to win.

Dia. 3 (Variation) If White answers at 2, Black moves back at 3 to live. Next, White A is countered by Black B, with no ko threats for White.

19

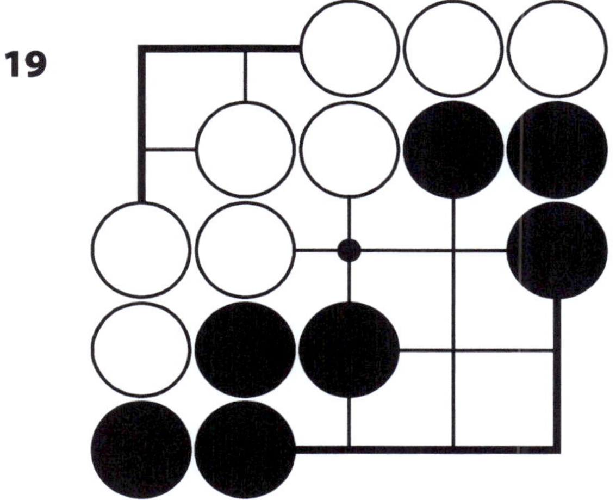

There is a way to live.

20

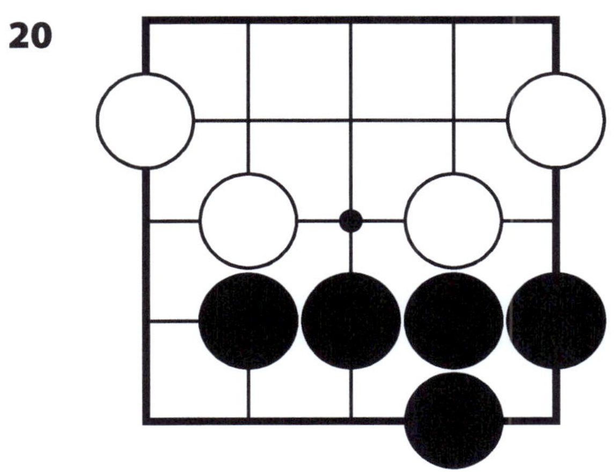

White's thin shape

Solution 19 **Black wins by two points.**

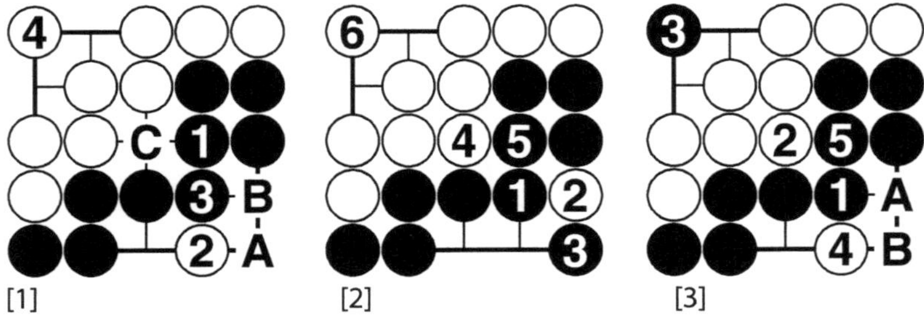

[1] [2] [3]

Dia. 1 (Failure) Black 1 is a bad choice. White 2 hits the vital point. After Black 3, White secures life with 4, but Black will die. Black lacks a ko threat to play A and White B. Black 3 at 4 is answered by White at 3. Black 1 at C is even worse as White counters at B.

Dia. 2 (Correct) Black 1 is a calm move. In the sequence from White 2 to 6 both sides live, but Black wins by two points.

Dia. 3 (Variation) If White answers at 2, Black 3 is sufficient. White 4 is fended off with Black 5. White has no ko threat to start the ko at A and Black B.

Solution 20 **Black wins by two points.**

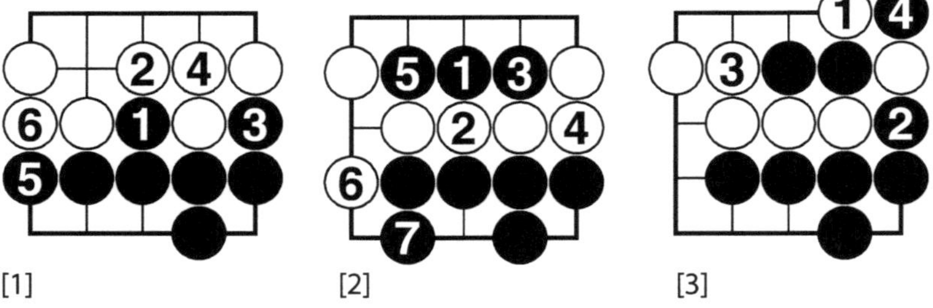

[1] [2] [3]

Dia. 1 (Failure) The simple endgame moves from Black 1 to 5 are not sufficient to win. After White 6, Black loses by two points.

Dia. 2 (Correct) Black 1 is a move right in the middle of White's position. After White 2, Black continues with 3 and 5, and creates a seki. If White plays 6, Black makes life with 7. Black wins by two points.

Dia. 3 (Variation) If White resists with 1 instead of 4 from the previous diagram, Black will cut at 2. White must play 3 and Black starts the ko at 4. But White lacks a ko threat, and so loses everything.

21

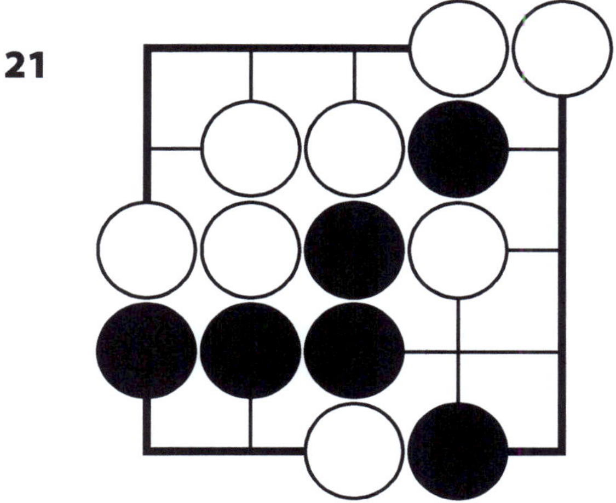

Make the other side defend

22

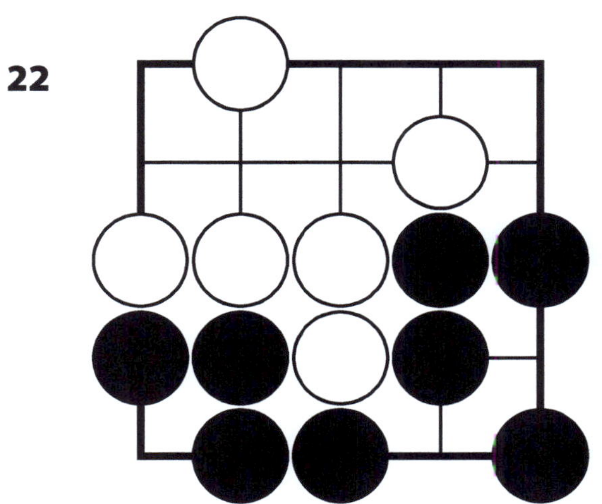

Leap a step forward

Solution 21 **Black wins by one point.**

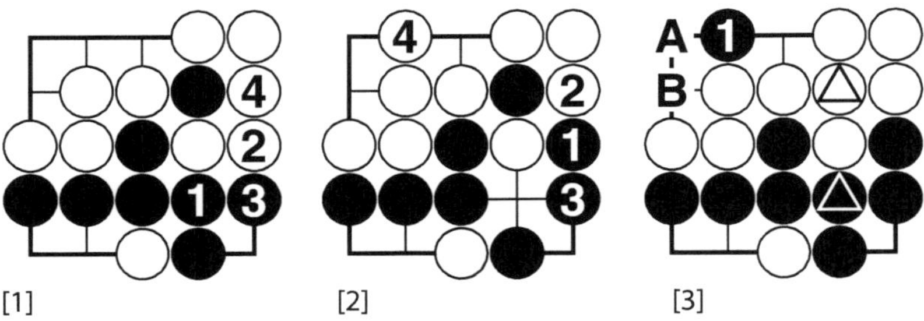

[1] [2] [3]

Dia. 1 (Failure) The game ends with Black 1 to White 4, but Black loses by two points. White 2 takes the crucial point.

Dia. 2 (Correct) Black 1 is a tesuji leaving White with no choice but to answer at 2. After Black 3, White must defend at 4 to live. Black wins by one point.

Dia. 3 (Variation) When White omits 4 in the previous diagram and the two marked stones have been played, Black can attack at 1. White has no ko threat to play A and Black B, hence he must defend in due time.

Solution 22 **Black wins by one point.**

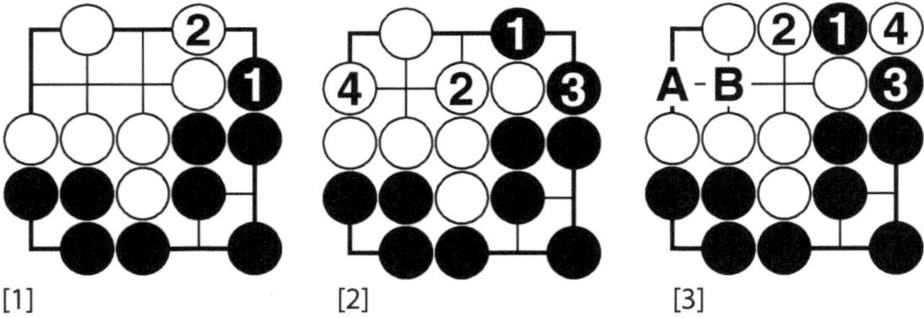

[1] [2] [3]

Dia. 1 (Failure) The game ends with Black 1 and White's extension to the edge at 2. Black loses by two points. White takes the crucial point in this position.

Dia. 2 (Correct) Black's clamp at 1 is the tesuji. White can only connect at 2, and Black turns at 3 reducing White's territory. Next White must make two eyes at 4. Thus Black wins by one point.

Dia. 3 (Variation) When White resists with 2, Black plays 3 in response. White 4 captures a stone starting a ko. Black will use A or B as a ko threat, but White has none. So Black will win the ko and the game.

23

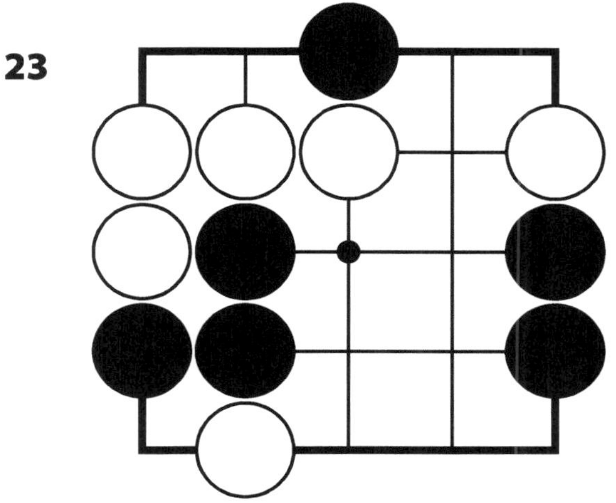

Far away

24

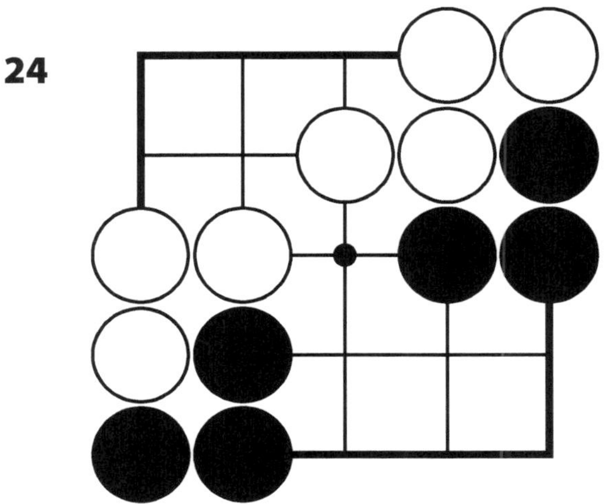

Mind the corner

Solution 23 **Black wins by one point.**

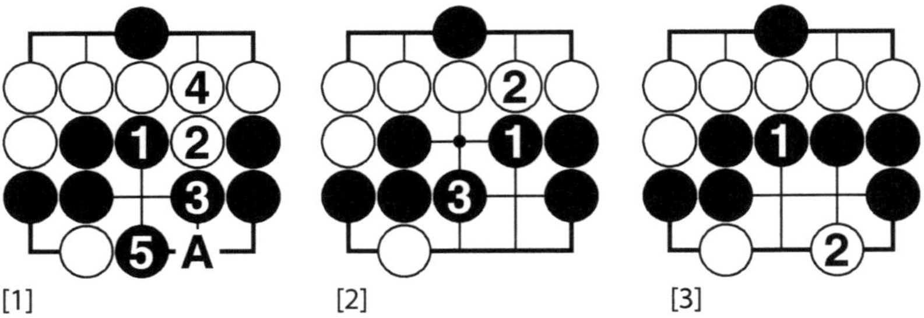

Dia. 1 (Failure) Black 1 is a failure because White pushes first at 2 and then connects at 4. Black's territory is still not safe as White A leads to a seki or ko. So Black needs to add another defensive move at 5. Both sides have six points now, the result is jigo.

Dia. 2 (Correct) Black 1 takes the key point. When White connects at 2, Black 3 is a good move without a need for additional defense. Black has seven points and wins the game by one.

Dia. 3 (Variation) Black must not be greedy and play 1 instead of 3 in the previous diagram. White counters at 2, turning the position into seki.

Solution 24 **Black wins by one point.**

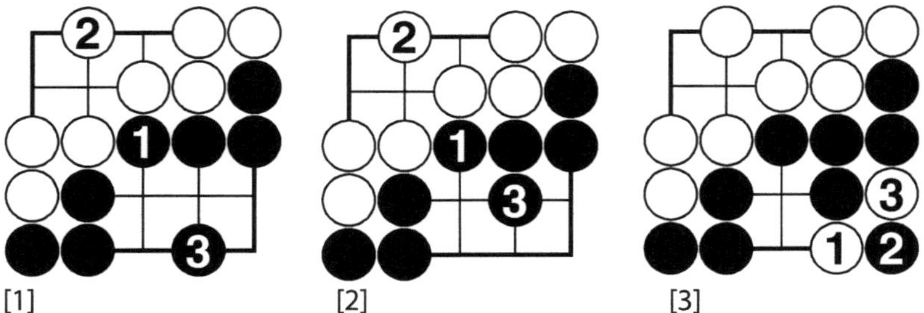

Dia. 1 (Correct) Black 1 threatens to cut and capture four stones, hence White must defend at 2. Black 3 secures the corner in proper shape. Now, there remains no aji in Black's corner. The result is a win by one point for Black.

Dia. 2 (Failure) Defending with Black 3 is a mistake. White will immediately take action to punish this move.

Dia. 3 (Continuation) White 1 hits the vital point. There is no choice but for Black to play 2 and start a ko. However, after White taking the ko, Black has no real ko threat.

25

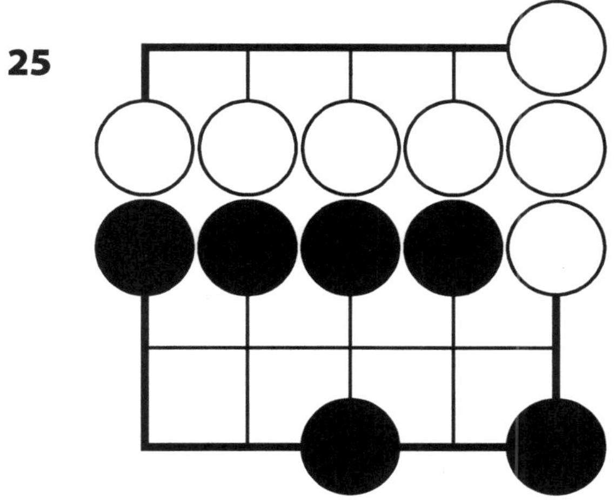

Don't mess up

26

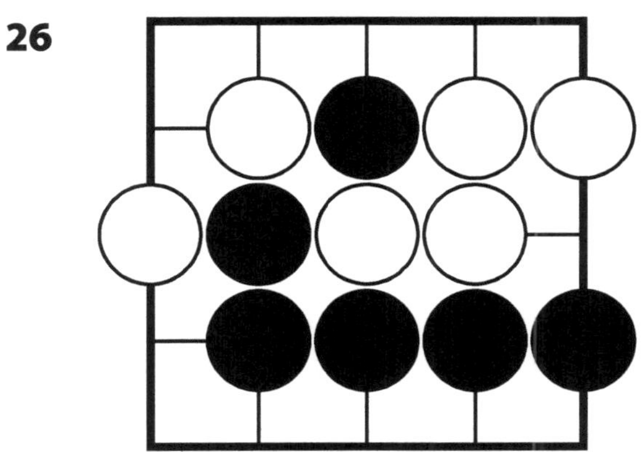

Aiming at ko

Solution 25 Black wins by three points.

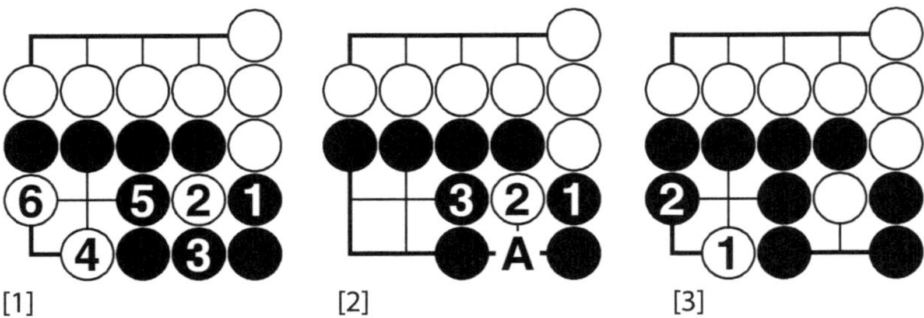

[1] [2] [3]

Dia. 1 (Failure) There is no move for Black inside White's area, hence the question is how Black can fence off his own position. Black 1 is the obvious choice, but it would be a mistake to play 3. Next, White 4 and 6 create a seki, and Black loses by three points.

Dia. 2 (Correct) After White 2, Black 3 is the correct answer. This way Black wins by three points. If White captures two stones at A, Black throws in at 1 to capture two stones in a snapback.

Dia. 3 (Reference) If White attacks at 1, Black 2 is good enough to defend.

Solution 26 Black wins by one point.

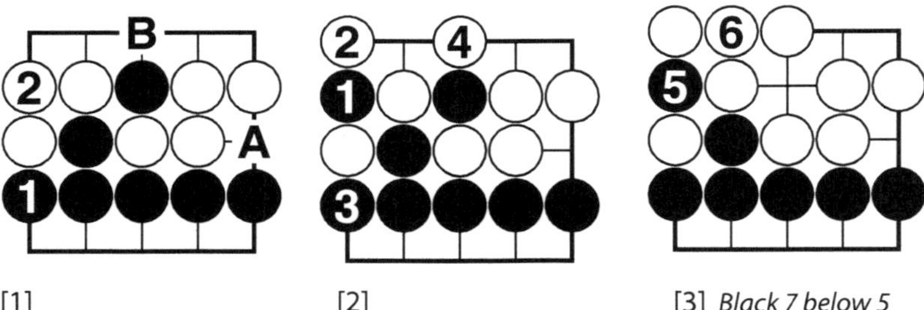

[1] [2] [3] *Black 7 below 5*

Dia. 1 (Failure) Simply blocking with Black 1 is a failure as White connects at 2. This is not enough to win the game. If Black plays A, White must defend at B. But still, Black has five points while White has six. Black loses by one point.

Dia. 2 (Correct) The only way to win is to play Black 1. White must capture with 2. After Black 3, White cannot connect at 1 but must first defend at 4.

Dia. 3 (Continuation) Next, Black 5 captures, White 6 connects, and Black finishes the ko with 7. Black wins by one point.

27

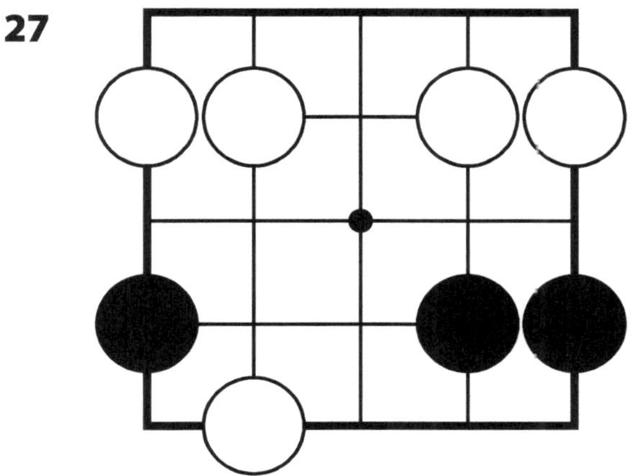

The key point

28

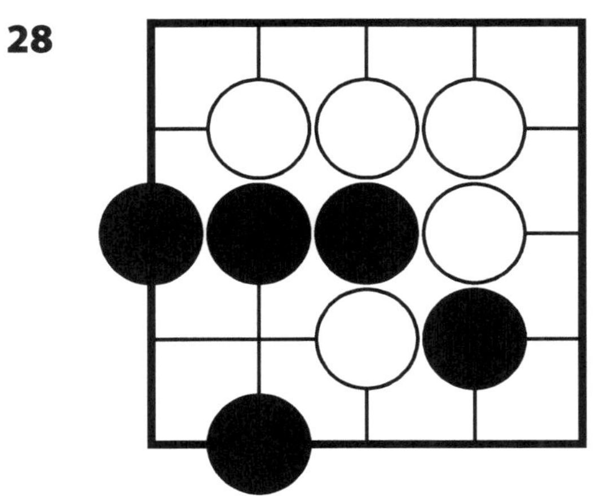

Play solidly

Solution 27 Black wins by one point.

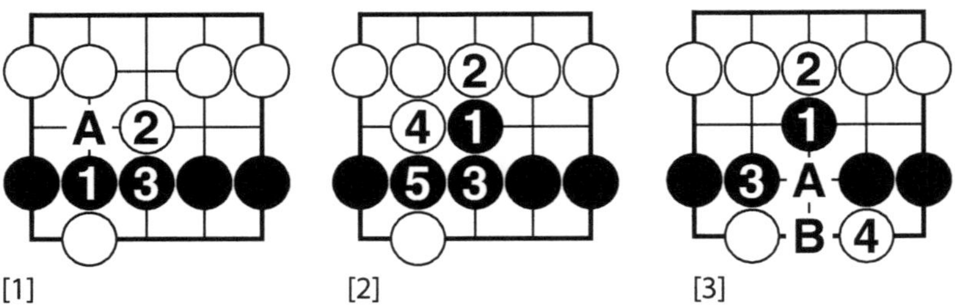

[1] [2] [3]

Dia. 1 (Failure) Black 1 is a failure. When White answers at 2, the game ends with Black 3. Both Black and White have six points. If Black plays 1 at A, White takes 2 again, and Black loses.

Dia. 2 (Correct) Black's kosumi at 1 is correct. This is the key point. After White connects at 2, Black 3 is now an important move. Black wins by one point.

Dia. 3 (Variation) If Black plays 3 on the second line, White counters at 4. Black has no choice but to play A, but White B creates a seki and Black loses. Black 3 is a failure.

Solution 28 Black wins by one point.

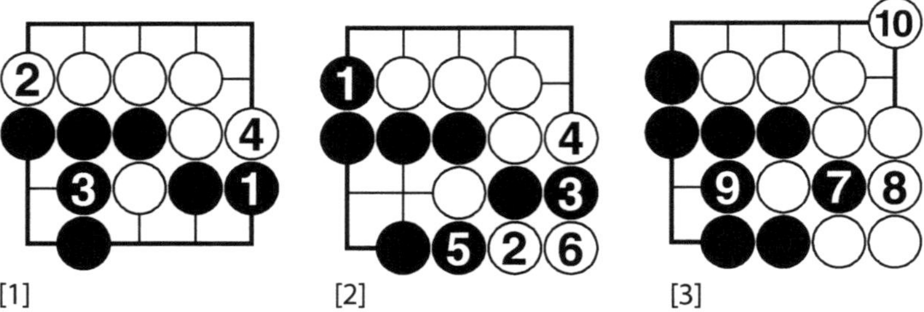

[1] [2] [3]

Dia. 1 (Correct) Black's extension at 1 is straightforward and the correct answer. White blocks at 2 and the game ends with 4. Black wins by one point.

Dia. 2 (Failure) Black's hane at 1 is a failure, because after White 2, Black is in trouble. Even if you try to play Black 3, White will erase the whole eye shape with 4 and 6. Black can't succeed. However, if White plays 2 at 3, Black wins...

Dia. 3 (Continuation) Even if Black throws in at 7 and connects at 9, White survives with 10, but Black is dead.

29

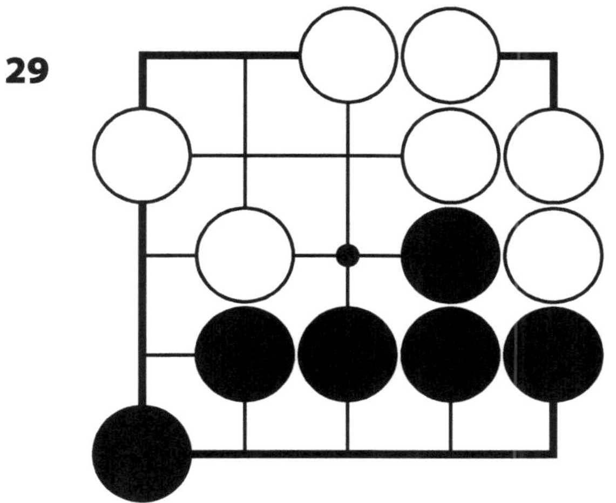

Read carefully

30

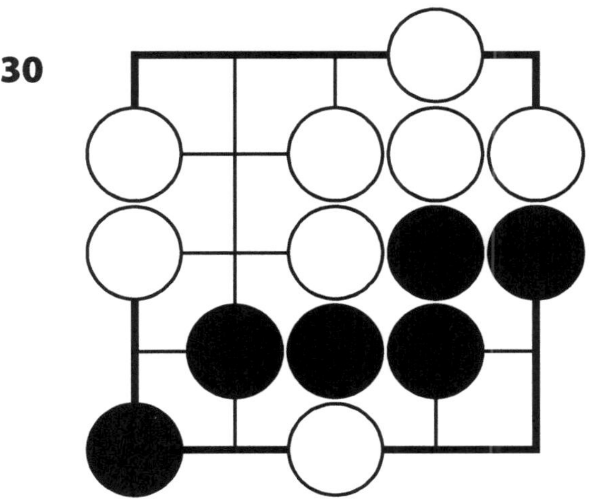

The problem is the third move

Solution 29 **Black wins by one point.**

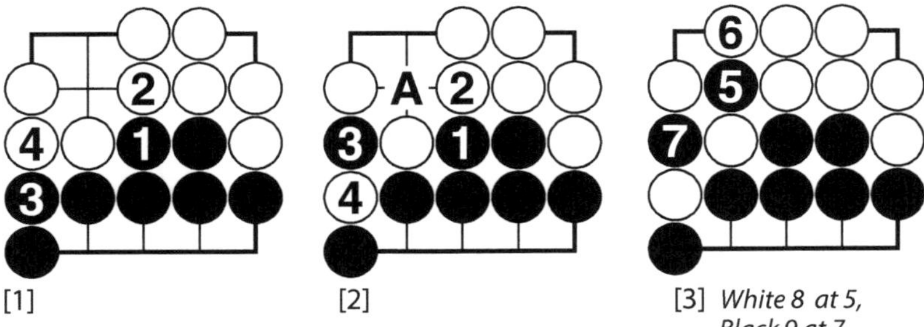

[1] [2] [3] *White 8 at 5, Black 9 at 7*

Dia. 1 (Failure) If Black plays 1 and 3 the game ends with White 4. This is a failure. You have to be more creative.

Dia. 2 (Correct) Starting a ko with Black 1 and 3 is a strong combination. Naturally, White takes with 4. If White connects with 4 at A, Black connects as well and wins by one point.

Dia. 3 (Continuation) After White has taken the ko, Black can play 5 as a ko threat. White 6 captures and Black 7 takes the ko again. White lacks a ko threat, so Black wins by one point.

Solution 30 **Black wins by one point.**

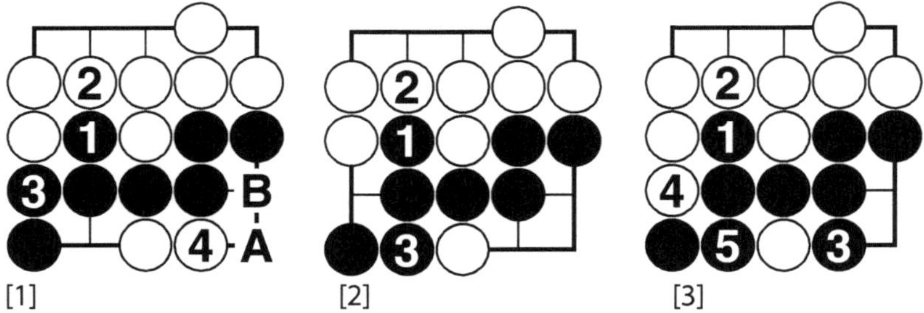

[1] [2] [3]

Dia. 1 (Failure) The first move must be Black 1, and White defends at 2. Next, the question is how to take care of Black's area. Black 3 is a failure, because White hits at 4. Black is forced to play a ko at A, but without ko threats he loses.

Dia. 2 (Correct) This Black 3 is the correct move to defend Black's territory. This move is good enough for Black to win by one point.

Dia. 3 (Failure) This Black 3 is a failure, as White can force with 4 from the outside. Now, Black must play another move to defend.

31

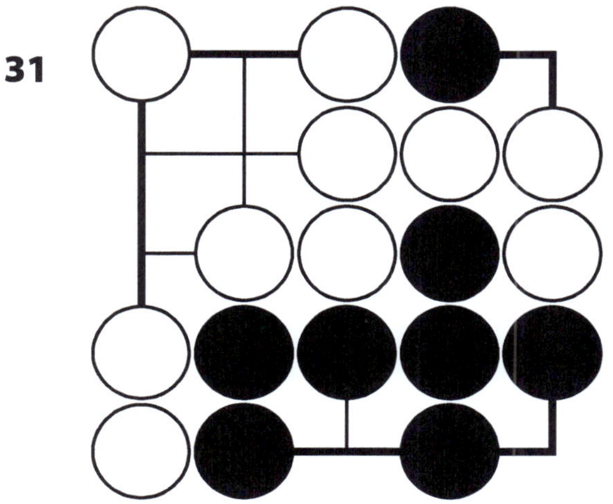

Pursuing sharply

32

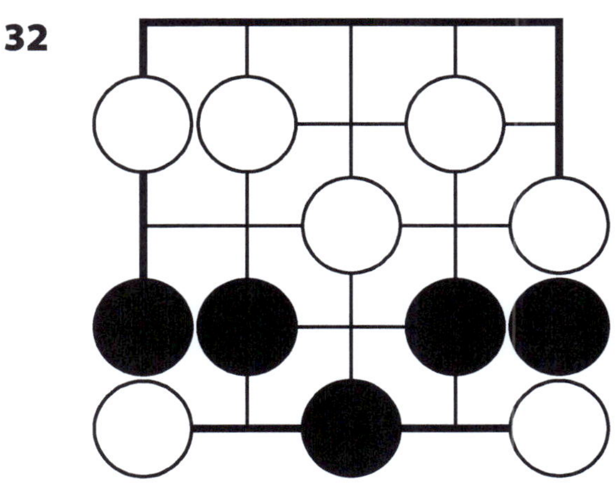

Lack of eyes

Solution 31 Black wins by two points.

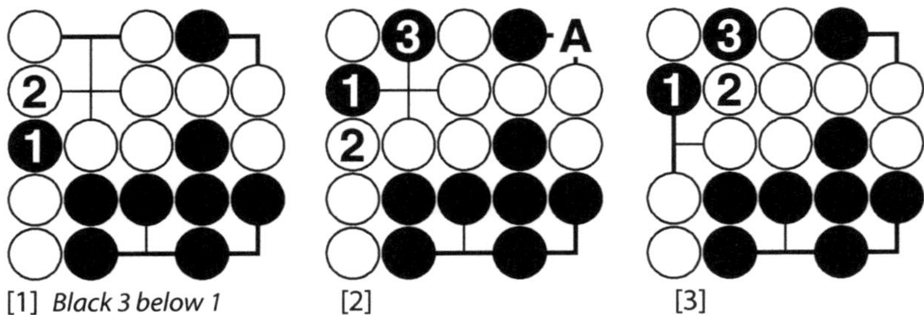

[1] *Black 3 below 1* [2] [3]

Dia. 1 (Failure) When Black captures two stones with 1, White will block at 2 and the game ends with Black's connection below 1. Black has four points all together, White has five.

Dia. 2 (Correct) Black 1 is a sharp move. If White connects with 2, Black correctly takes a stone at 3. White cannot approach and is left to capture a stone at A. White lives in seki, so Black wins by two points.

Dia. 3 (Variation) If White plays 2, Black will capture at 3. White has no ko threat, so he dies.

Solution 32 Black wins by one point.

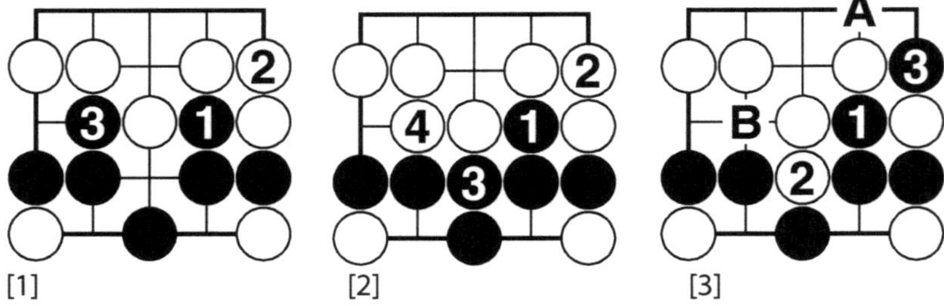

[1] [2] [3]

Dia. 1 (Correct) Black must play atari at 1. After White connects at 2, Black continues straight ahead with 3 and wins by one point. There is no defensive move needed inside of Black's area.

Dia. 2 (Failure) After White 2, it is bad to connect with Black 3. White takes the key point at 4, thus has a larger territory. The result of the game is turned into jigo. If Black starts with 1 at 4, White will push at 3 and Black loses by three points.

Dia. 3 (Variation) If White answers Black 1 with the push at 2, Black first takes a stone with 3. Next, if White A and Black B, then White dies.

33

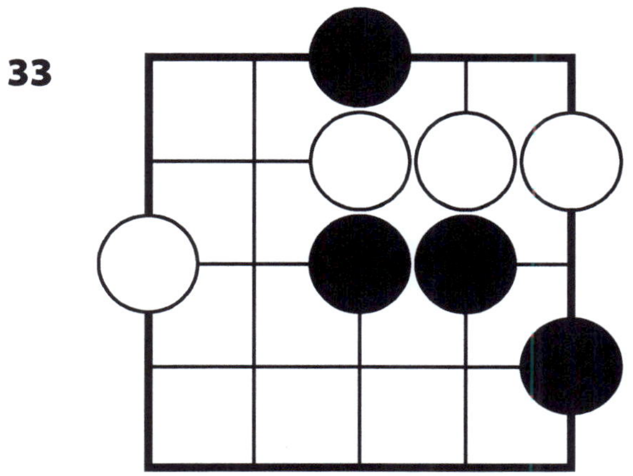

How to protect

34

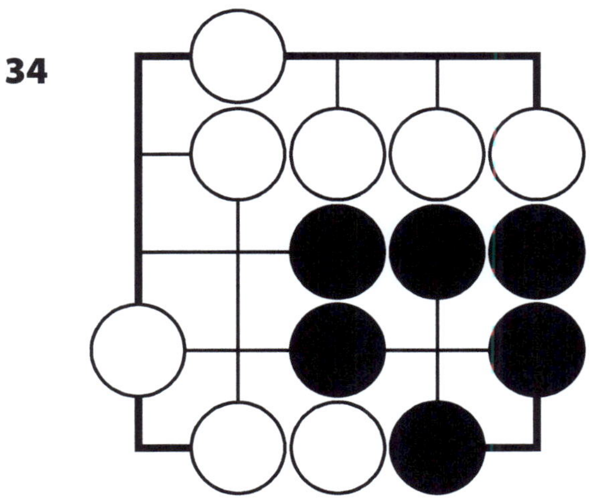

How to take advantage

Solution 33 **Black wins by one point.**

[1] [2] [3]

Dia. 1 (Correct) Black 1 and 3 are natural moves. The key to the game is Black 5. Any other way would require one more move. Black wins by one point. If Black plays 1 at 2, White will cut off the stone with 1 and Black loses.

Dia. 2 (Failure) Black's throw-in at 3 is terrible as White will push at 4. In the end Black loses by one point.

Dia. 3 (Failure) Instead of 7 in the previous diagram, if Black attacks at 1, White will counter with 2 to 8. Black may capture two stones, but White will retake one. In the end, the result is jigo.

Solution 34 **Black wins by one point.**

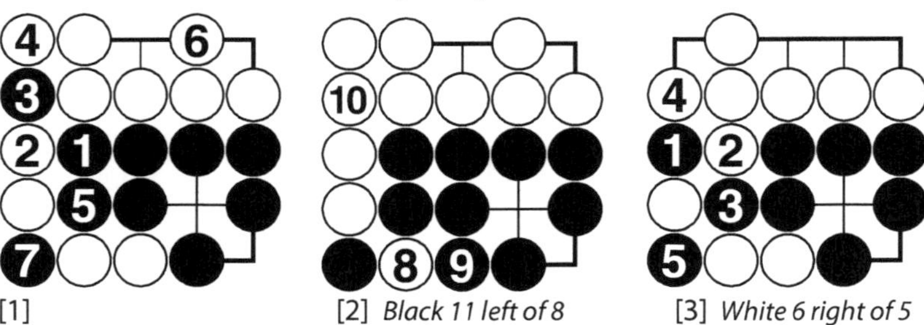

[1] [2] *Black 11 left of 8* [3] *White 6 right of 5*

Dia. 1 (Correct) It is a good idea to simply play Black 1. When White answers at 2, Black throws in at 3. White takes, and Black squeezes from the outside with 5. Now White must make two eyes with 6, and Black captures two stones...

Dia. 2 (Continuation) Next, White takes a stone with 8, and Black blocks at 9. As White cannot connect, Black captures again with 11 (left of 8). There is no ko threat, so Black will connect the ko and win by one point.

Dia. 3 (Failure) Black 1 is a mistake in this case. White answers with 2 and 4, making a big life. Black loses by one point.

35

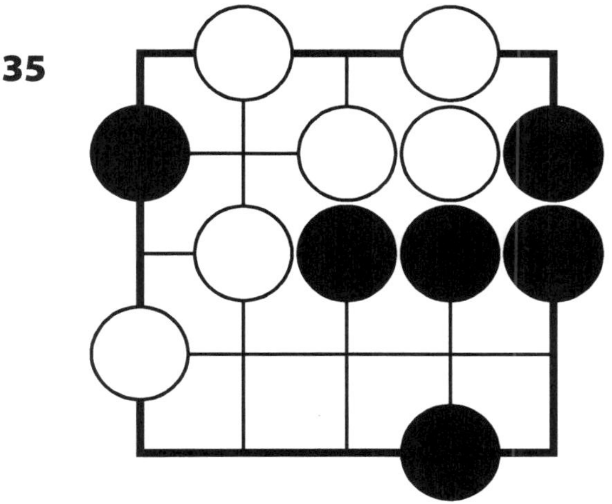

Aiming at a one point win

36

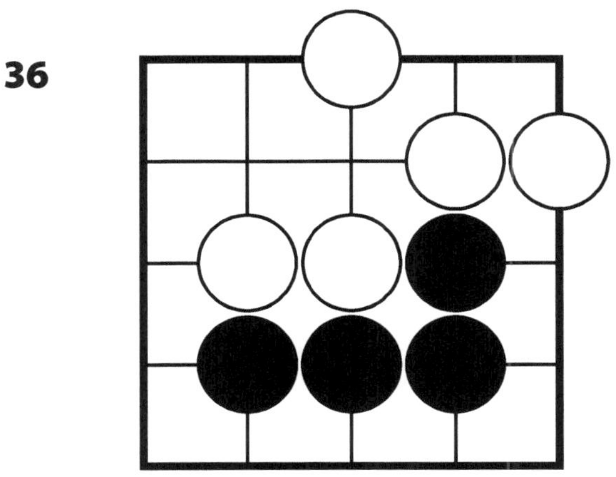

Sente and gote

Solution 35 **Black wins by two points.**

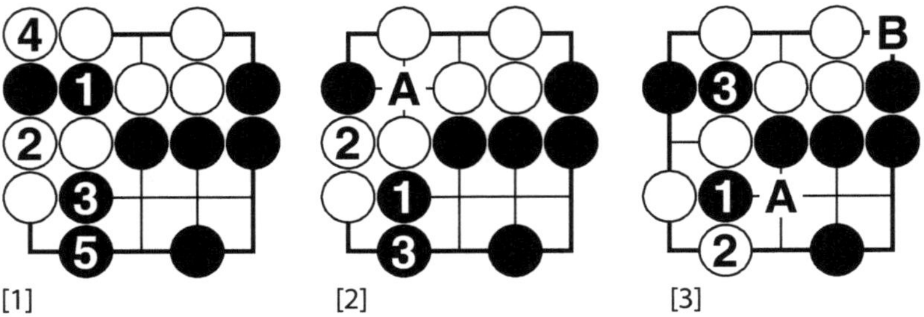

[1] [2] [3]

Dia. 1 (Failure) Black 1 looks like a strong tesuji and Black makes use of the sacrificed stones. However, at the end of the game, both Black and White have five points of territory. Thus, this is a failure.

Dia. 2 (Correct) The trick is to keep the cut at A open. The correct way is simply blocking with Black 1 and White answers with 2. In the end, White even has to connect at A and Black wins by one point.

Dia. 3 (Variation) If White answers with the atari 2, Black will cut at 3. When White takes a stone at A, Black captures three stones with B.

Solution 36 **Black wins by one point.**

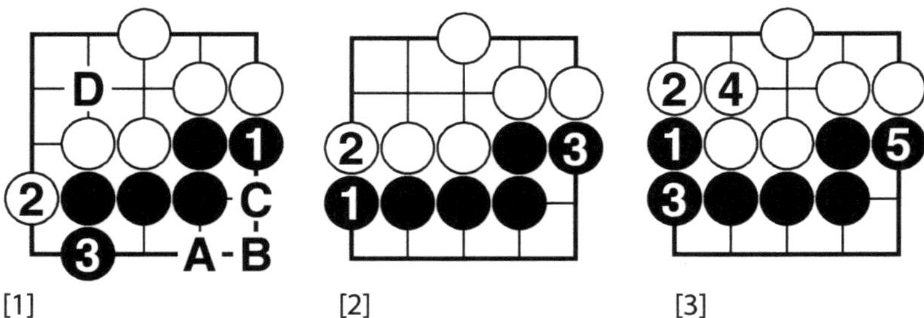

[1] [2] [3]

Dia. 1 (Failure) Blocking with Black 1 is wrong. White 2 is good enough. Black 3 surrounds four points, but there is still a weakness at A. Next, White removes the ko threat at D and Black defends inside his area against the sequence White A, Black B and White C.

Dia. 2 (Failure) Black 1 here gains more territory, but it is still not enough to win. Black loses by one point.

Dia. 3 (Correct) Black's hane and connect with 1 and 3 are correct, followed by Black 5. Black wins by one point.

37

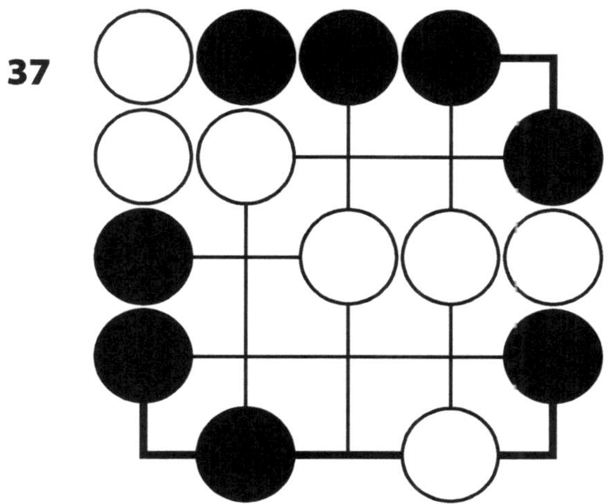

How to decide

38

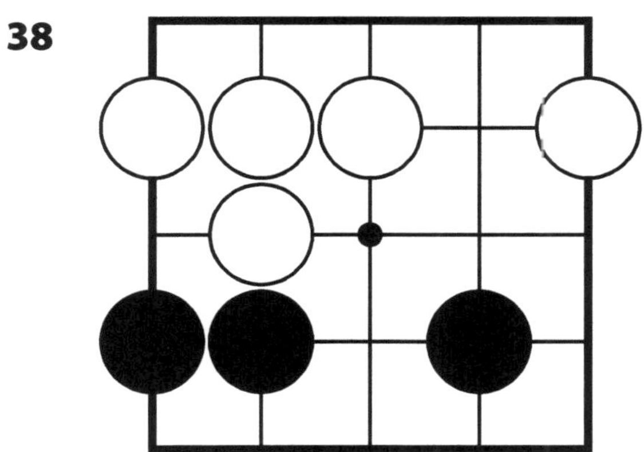

The endgame key point is where?

Solution 37 **Black wins by one point.**

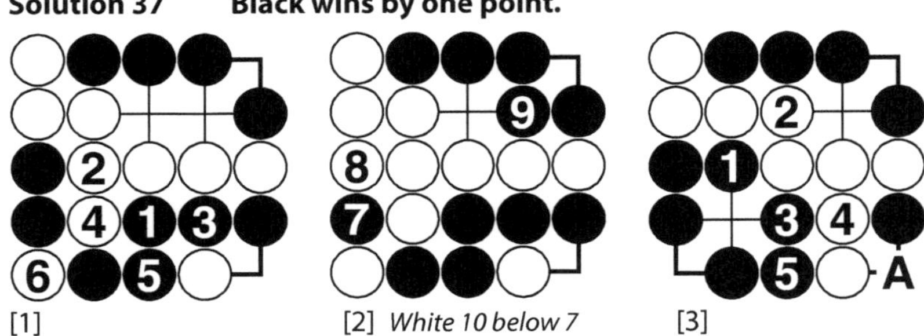
[1] [2] *White 10 below 7* [3]

Dia. 1 (Failure) Black's kosumi at 1 is not good because White answers at 2. Even if Black connects with 3, White will push at 4. After Black 5, White captures two stones with 6.

Dia. 2 (Continuation) Next, Black 7 and 9, White 10 will take the ko again. Black has no ko threat and dies.

Dia. 3 (Correct) The correct answer is to be straightforward and make life with Black 1 to 5. Black's four stones at the top work, creating a seki. White can capture a stone at A, but Black still wins by one point.

Solution 38 **Black wins by one point.**

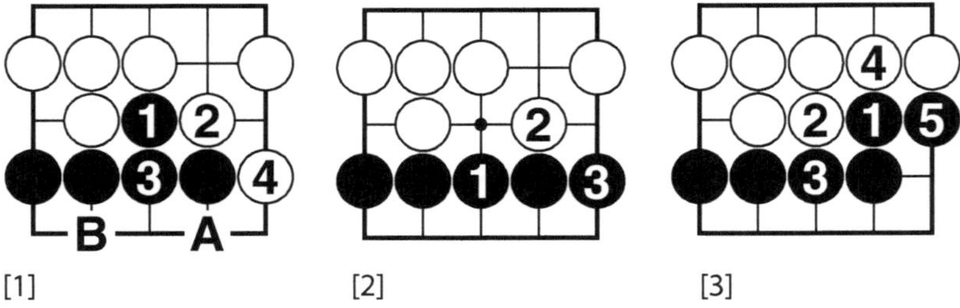
[1] [2] [3]

Dia. 1 (Failure) Black 1 is a bad move. White 2 forces Black to play 3, and White 4 kills Black. If Black A, White B takes the vital point.

Dia. 2 (Failure) Connecting with Black 1 is a solid move, but White 2 increases White's score by one point. Black loses by one point.

Dia. 3 (Correct) Black 1 is the vital point and increases Black's territory. Next, White 2 to Black 5 finish the game. Black wins by one point. The same result applies if White plays 2 at 4.

39

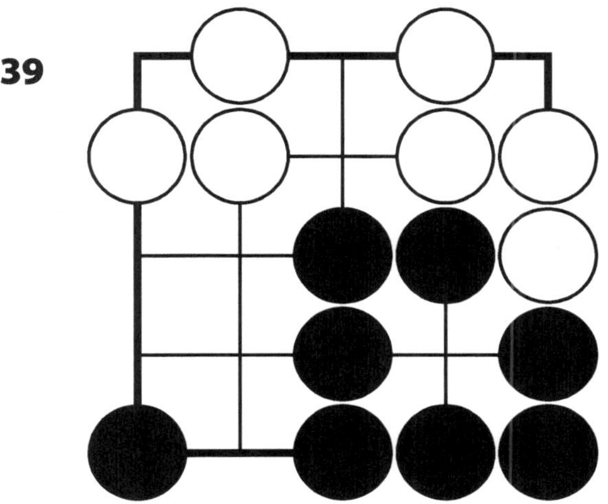

Mind the counter

40

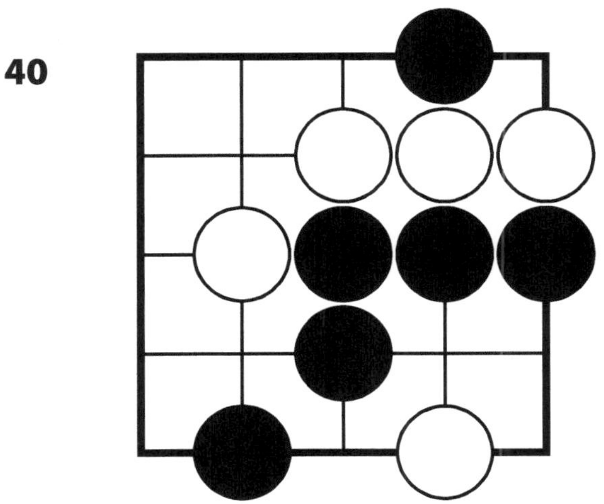

Make an eye in the corner

Solution 39 Black wins by one point.

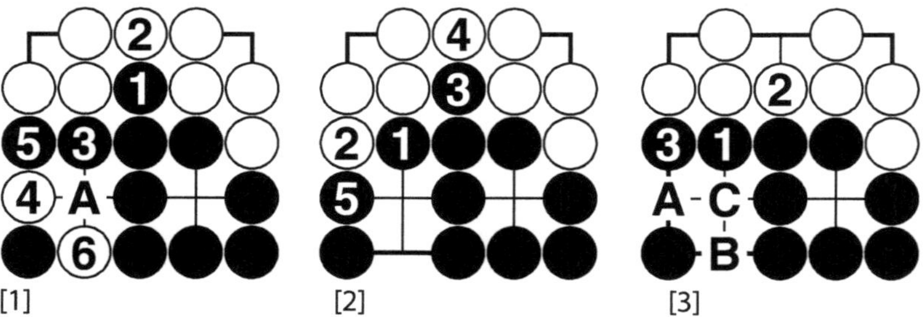

Dia. 1 (Failure) It's tempting to play Black 1, but this is a bad move. If Black continues with 3, White will counter with 4. After Black 5 and White 6, Black has only achieved a seki and will lose. If Black plays 3 at A or 4, the final result will be jigo.

Dia. 2 (Correct) It's correct to simply play the block at 1. When White pushes at 2, Black can play 3. After 5, Black wins by one point.

Dia. 3 (Variation) If White answers at 2, White still has one point less than Black. If White plays 2 at A, the sequence Black 3, White B and Black C will follow.

Solution 40 Black wins by one point.

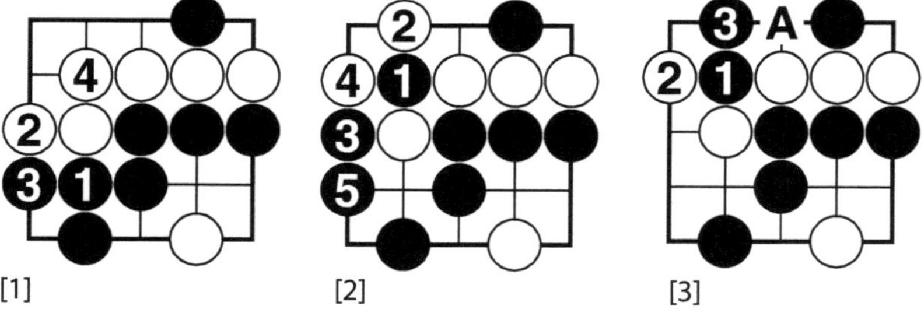

Dia. 1 (Failure) Black 1 is not enough. White answers at 2 and connects at 4. The same happens if Black plays 3 first. White will answer at 2, followed by Black 1 and White 4. Black cannot win this way.

Dia. 2 (Correct) Black's sacrifice at 1 is a good move. White plays the atari 2. Black 3 forces White to capture, then Black extends to 5. Now, White only has six points, and Black wins by one point.

Dia. 3 (Variation) White cannot play the atari from the other side as his position collapses after Black extends at 3. White cannot approach at A.

41

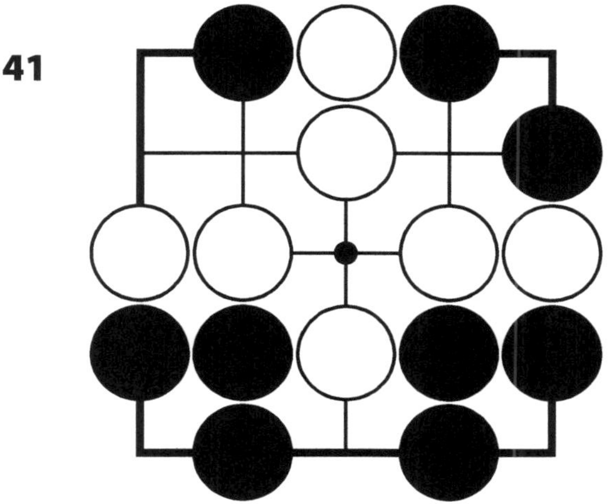

A subtle neutral point

42

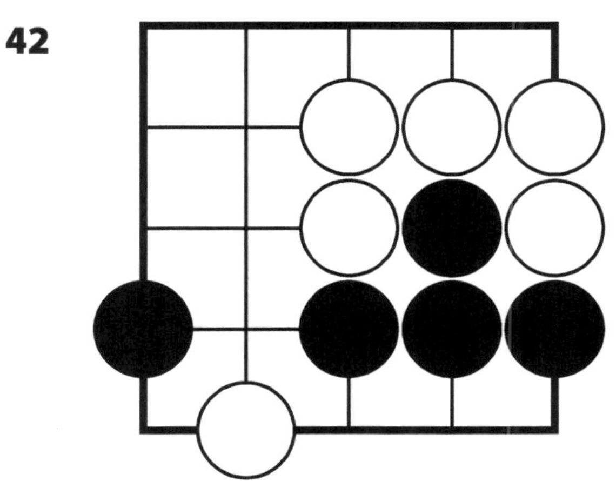

One line difference

Solution 41 **Black wins by two points.**

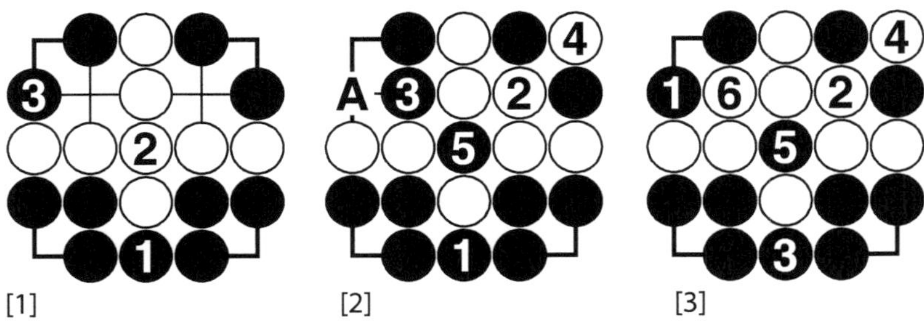

Dia. 1 (Correct) There is no choice but to play Black 1. White has to play 2. Black 3, creating a seki, is the winning move.

Dia. 2 (Variation) This move 2 does not work for White. Black plays the atari at 3, White must capture at 4, and Black plays 5. Black will win the ko and capture two more stones a A. This is a big difference.

Dia. 3 (Failure) Black 1 is the wrong order as it allows White to play 2 and 4. After Black 5, White can play 6 and Black has gained nothing. Instead, he loses by seven points.

Solution 42 **Black wins by one point.**

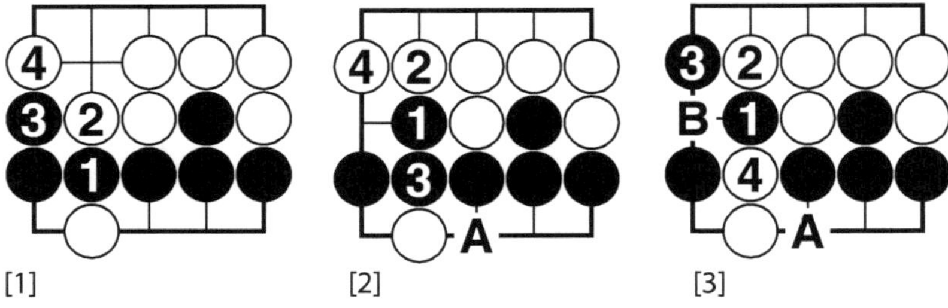

Dia. 1 (Failure) Black's connection at 1 is a straightforward move that reinforces the decisive point, but after White blocks at 2, both sides end up with six points. Jigo is a failure.

Dia. 2 (Correct) It is correct to bend at 1, thus reducing White's territory by one point. The game ends with White 2 to 4. Black wins by one point. If White plays 2 at 3, Black defends at A.

Dia. 3 (Variation) Black 3 is greedy. White counters at 4 and Black is in trouble. After Black A, White will take at B. Since there is no ko threat, Black will lose. If Black plays B first, White will play A.

43

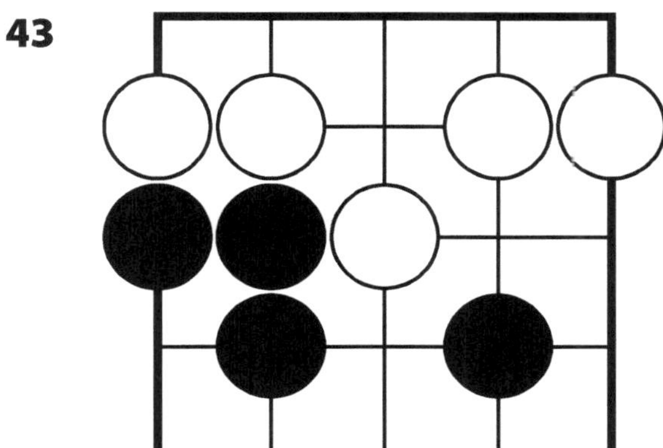

The key point is here!

44

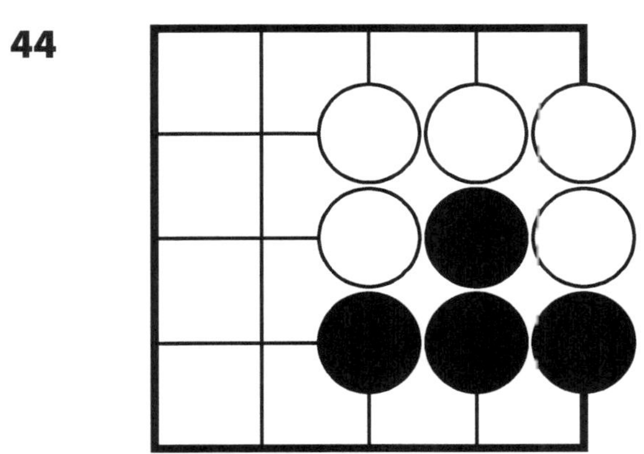

A question of attention

Solution 43 Black wins by one point.

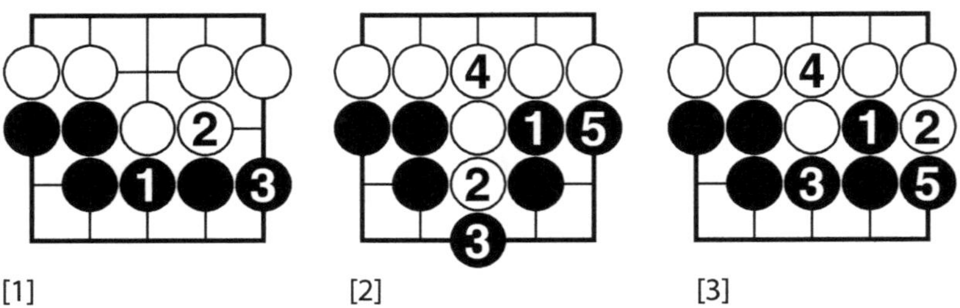

[1] [2] [3]

Dia. 1 (Failure) Connecting with Black 1 is a natural move to stop White, but it lacks ingenuity. After White 2 and Black 3 the game ends with six points for both Black and White. But jigo is a failure for Black.

Dia. 2 (Correct) Black 1 is the critical point, reducing White's area by one point and helping to increase Black's own area. When White pushes at 2, Black blocks first at 3 and then at 5. Black wins by one point.

Dia. 3 (Variation) If White plays 2 first, the result will be the same with Black 3 to 5.

Solution 44 Black wins by one point.

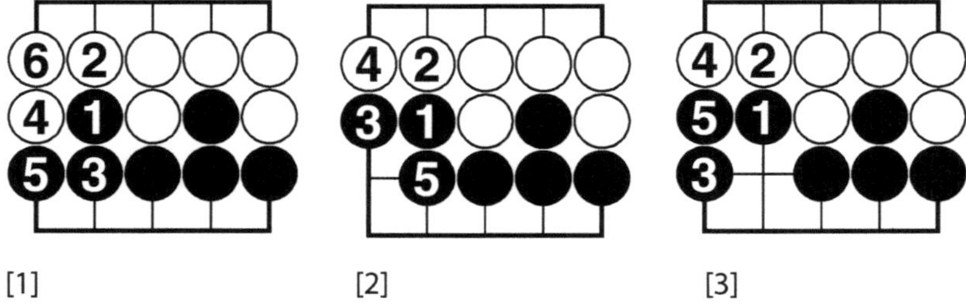

[1] [2] [3]

Dia. 1 (Failure) Black 1 is a basic endgame move. It's important to be careful when White blocks at 2. It's not a good idea to make another regular move with Black 3. After White 4 to 6, both sides have five points.

Dia. 2 (Correct) The correct answer is to extend to 3 and to not allow White the hane and connection on the first line. This time, Black wins by one point.

Dia. 3 (Correct) The hanging connection of Black 3 is also correct. White 4 and Black 5 end the game with a win for Black.

Chapter 2: STEP

Black to play and win!

1

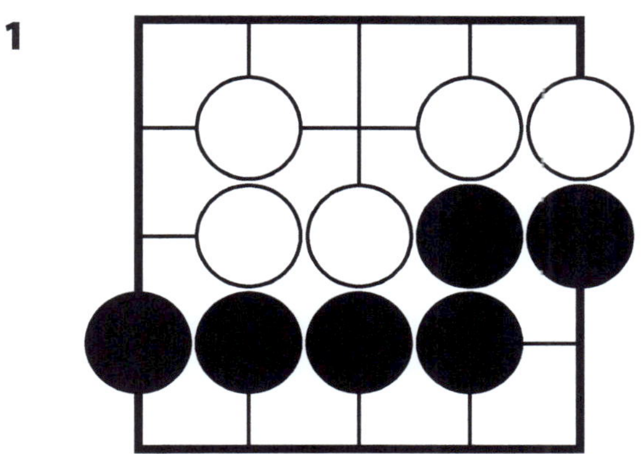

A blow to the vital point

2

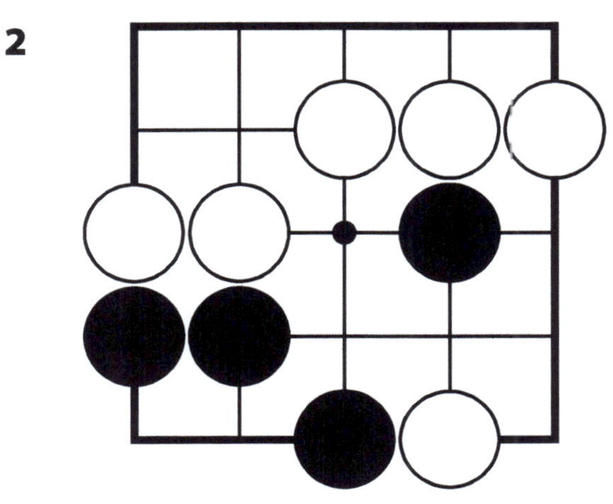

If you fail, White wins

Solution 1 **Black wins by two points.**

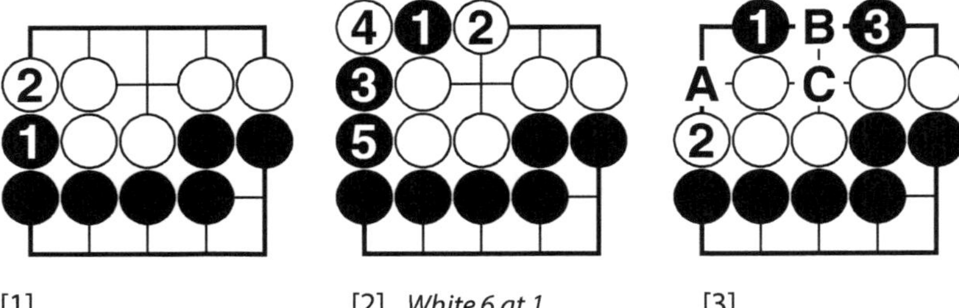

[1] [2] *White 6 at 1* [3]

Dia. 1 (Failure) When Black simply pushes at 1, the game ends with White's block at 2. Each side has six points of territory, but jigo is a failure for Black.

Dia. 2 (Correct) Black's attachment at 1 is tesuji. If White answers at 2, Black plays 3 and 5. After White connects with 6 at 1, Black wins by two points.

Dia. 3 (Variation) When White answers at 2 or at A, Black plays 3. White can live in seki with no points to count. Starting a ko with B is worse as White has no ko threat after Black captures at C.

Solution 2 **Black wins by one point.**

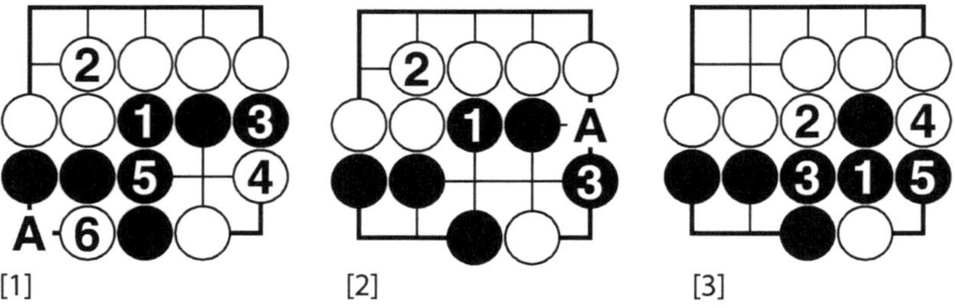

[1] [2] [3]

Dia. 1 (Failure) Choosing Black 1 is fine, but extending to 3 is a mistake. White 4 threatens a snapback, and then White 6 creates a seki. After capturing a stone at A, Black has only one point while White has six.

Dia. 2 (Correct) Black 3 takes the critical point. Even though White will take the point at A, Black must not defend anymore. Thus Black wins by one point.

Dia. 3 (Failure) Black 1 here is a poor move leaving the points 2 and 4 to White. In the end, Black loses by two points.

3

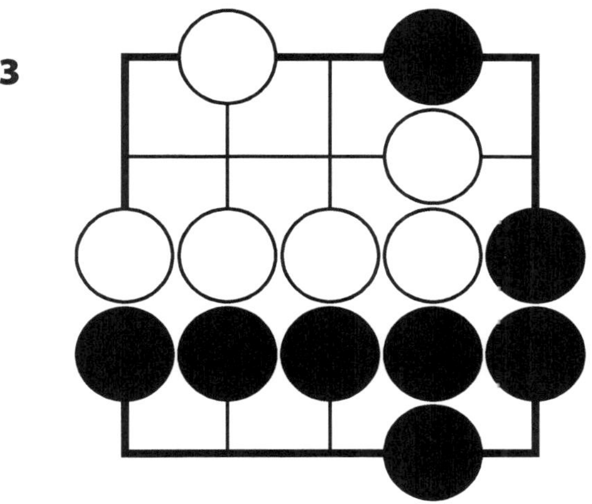

Go a step further

4

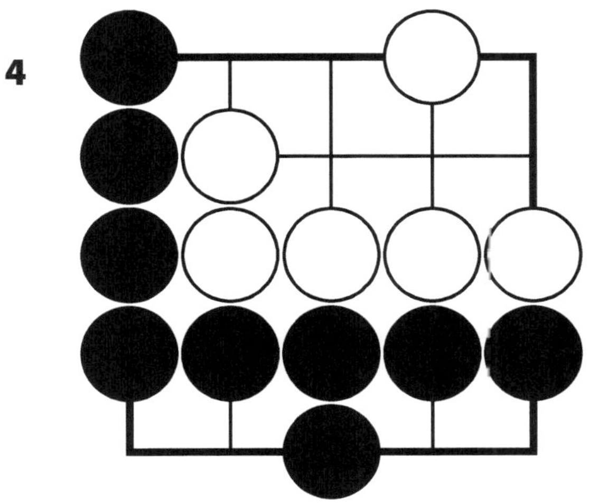

A bad idea

Solution 3 **Black wins by one point.**

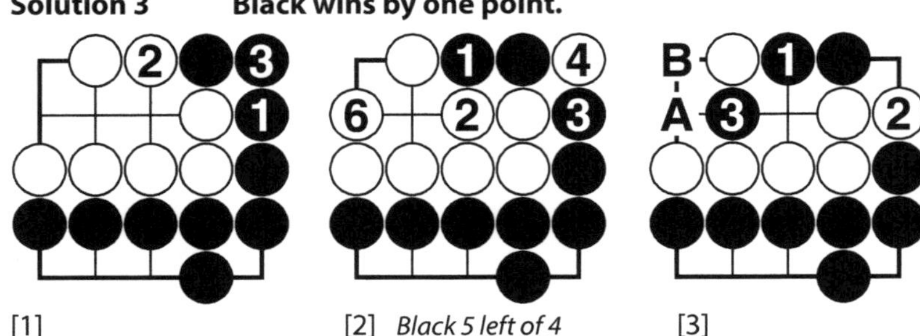

[1] [2] *Black 5 left of 4* [3]

Dia. 1 (Failure) If Black plays 1, White will simply answer at 2 and Black connects at 3. This is normal, but jigo is a failure for Black.

Dia. 2 (Correct) Black 1 is a clever move. After White 2 to 4, Black captures the white stone with 5. Now, White must defend at 6 to make two eyes. Black wins by one point.

Dia. 3 (Variation) If Black 1 is answered by White 2, Black can start a ko at 3. After White A, Black takes at B. Since White has no ko threat, Black will connect and the position is turned into a seki.

Solution 4 **Black wins by one point.**

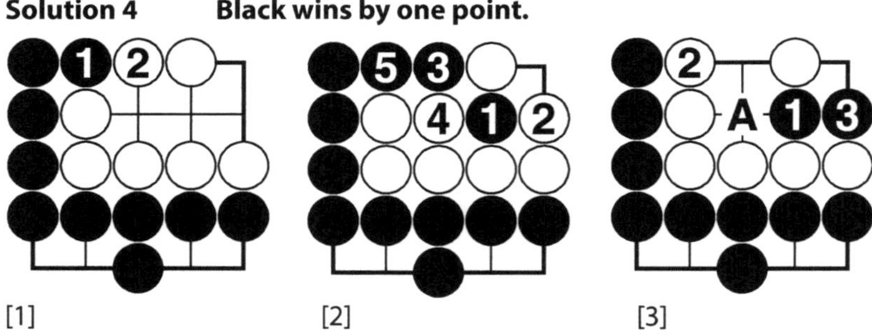

[1] [2] [3]

Dia. 1 (Failure) It seems that there is no choice but for Black to play 1. White finishes the game with 2, and the result is jigo, a failure for Black.

Dia. 2 (Correct) Black 1 is a sharp move. White's answer at 2 is correct. Now Black plays atari at 3 and connects at 5. This way Black wins by one point.

Dia. 3 (Failure) If White answers Black 1 with 2, Black extends at 3. White cannot play A because of shortage of liberties. Even if White plays at A instead of 2, Black will kill with 3. White is dead.

5

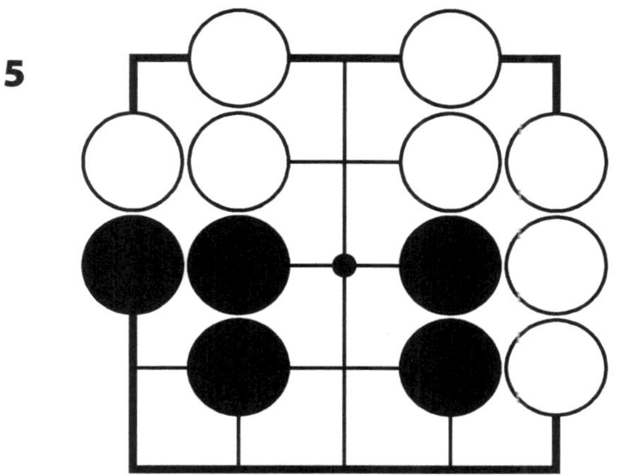

Temptation

6

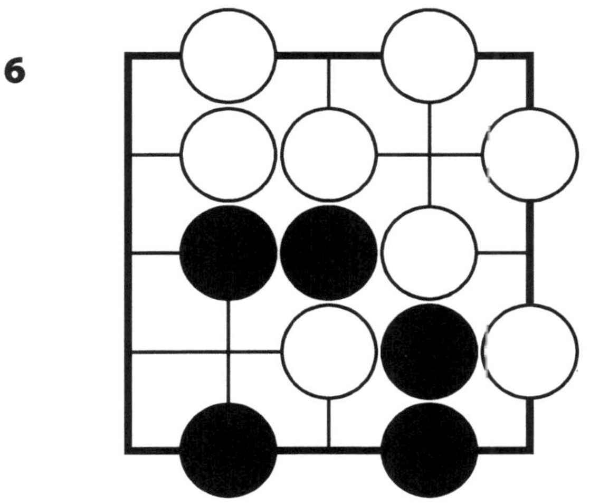

Be on your guard

Solution 5 Black wins by two points.

[1] [2] [3]

Dia. 1 (Correct) The correct answer is to block the territory at 1. White blocks as well at 2, and with Black 3 the game ends. If White plays 2 at 3, then Black will take 2. White must defend at A, Black blocks at B, and White connects at C. Still, the result is a win for Black by two points.

Dia. 2 (Failure) Black 1 is greedy, and is quickly outplayed by White 2. After Black 3 and White 4, Black dies.

Dia. 3 (Failure) If Black considers safety first and secures eye shape at 1, White can push at 2. This way the game ends in jigo.

Solution 6 Black wins by one point.

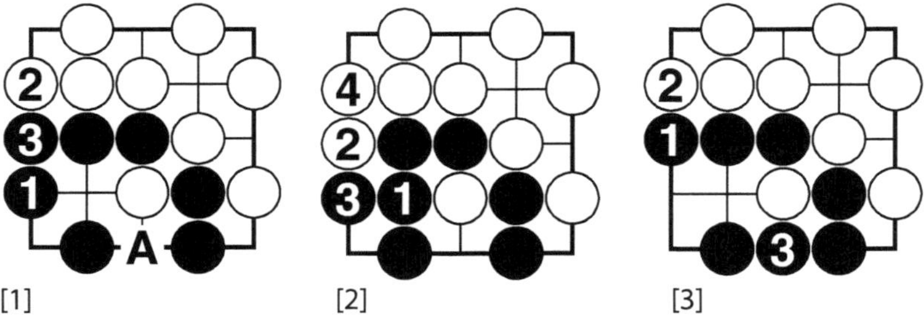

[1] [2] [3]

Dia. 1 (Failure) Black 1 is a poor move. After White 2 and Black 3, the game ends in jigo. At the end, Black still must connect at A.

Dia. 2 (Failure) Black 1 here is even worse. This move is countered by White 2. Black has now lost an additional point.

Dia. 3 (Correct) Extending with Black 1 is correct. After 3, Black will not need to defend any further. Black wins by one point.

7

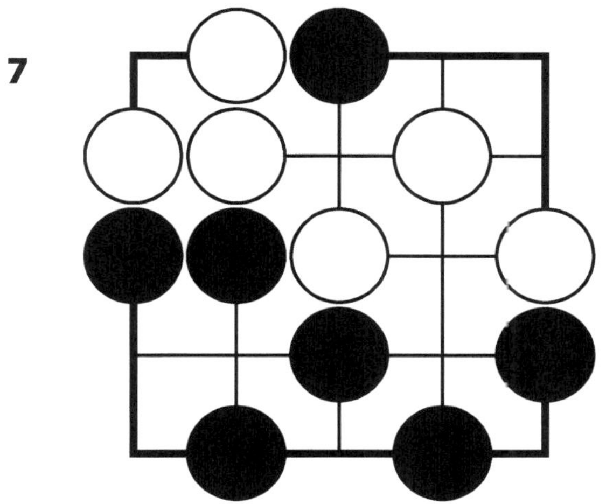

It must be ko

8

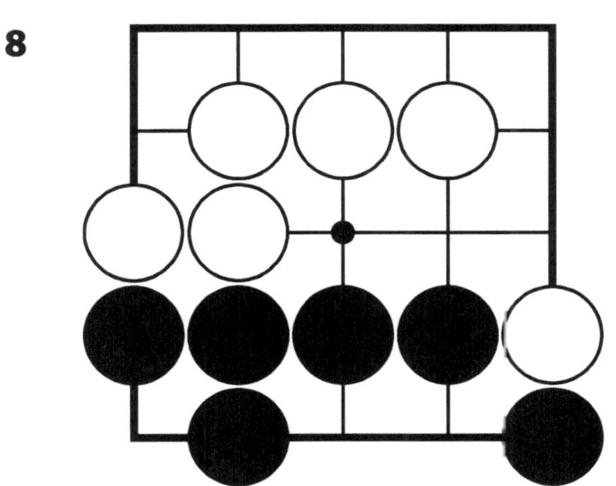

Capture a white stone, but...

Solution 7 Black wins by three points.

[1] [2] [3]

Dia. 1 (Failure) The game ends here with Black 1 and White 2, which is a bit uninspired. Black loses by two points. Black can do more.

Dia. 2 (Correct) The only way to win, is starting a ko by throwing in with Black 1. After White captures with 2, Black 3 serves as a suitable ko threat. White must answer at 4.

Dia. 3 (Continuation) When Black continues with 5 and 7, Black wins by three points.

Solution 8 Black wins by one point.

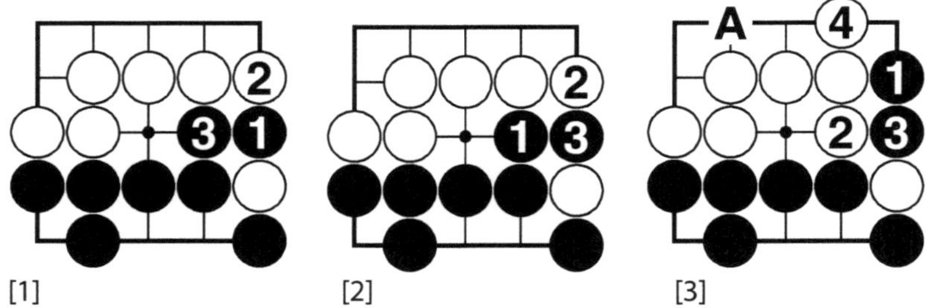

[1] [2] [3]

Dia. 1 (Failure) The most common move would be Black 1. However, after White 2 and Black 3, Black loses by one point.

Dia. 2 (Failure) Black 1 will be answered by White 2 again. The result is the same as in the previous diagram.

Dia. 3 (Correct) The clever move is the jump to 1. White has no choice but to play 2 and 4. Since there is a weak point at A, White must add another defensive move inside. In the end, Black has four points and White three. With the correct answer, Black wins by one point.

9

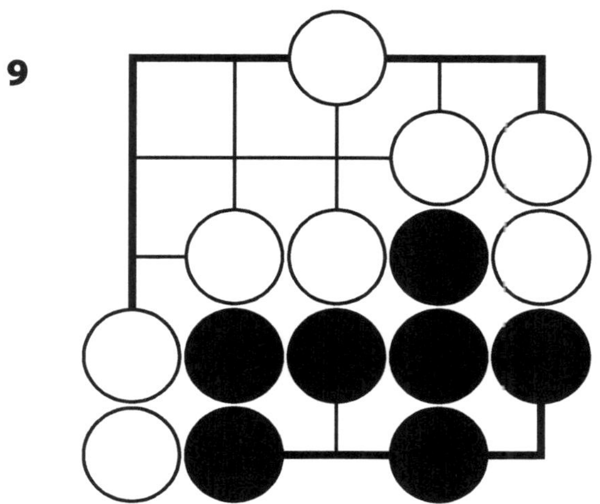

You want to take them

10

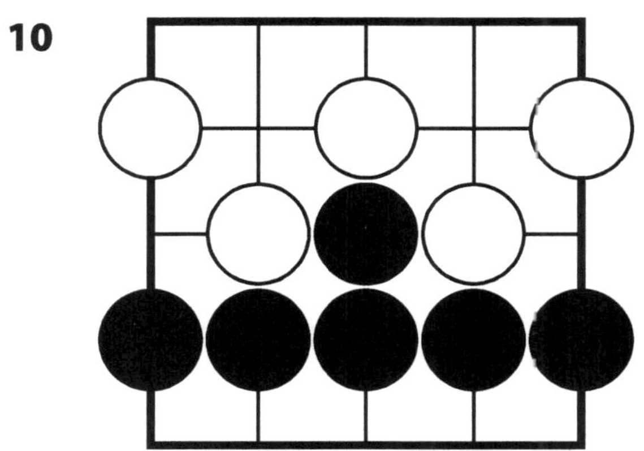

The ordinary endgame...

Solution 9 **Black wins by one point.**

[1] *Black 3 below 1* [2] [3]

Dia. 1 (Failure) Capturing with Black 1 and blocking at White 2 are the usual way of play. The game ends with Black connecting below 1 and White connecting at 4. The result is jigo.

Dia. 2 (Correct) Black 1 is the tesuji. Black 3 to 5 create a seki inside of White's territory. White has one stone captured, so Black wins by one point. If Black omits to play 5, White will win with a move at A.

Dia. 3 (Failure) Black 1 fails due to White 2.

Solution 10 **Black wins by five points.**

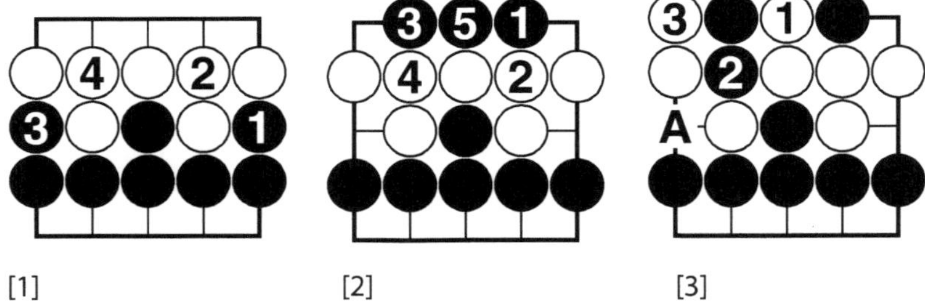

[1] [2] [3]

Dia. 1 (Failure) It would be a normal sequence to end the game with Black 1 to White 4. However, this is a failure. Both Black and White end up with five points each.

Dia. 2 (Correct) There are weak points within White's area. Black 1 and 3 is a good way to play. After Black 5, the position is seki and Black wins by five points.

Dia. 3 (Variation) Instead of White 4 in the previous diagram, White may play 1. Black counters with 2, and after White 3, Black throws in at 2 again. White has captured some stones, but the position is dead.

11

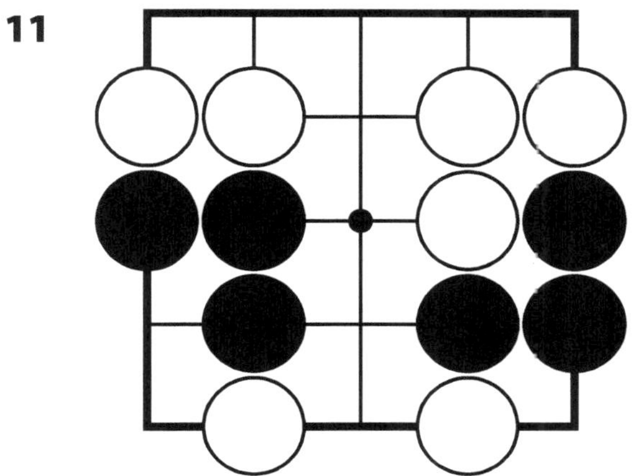

Choose from two options

12

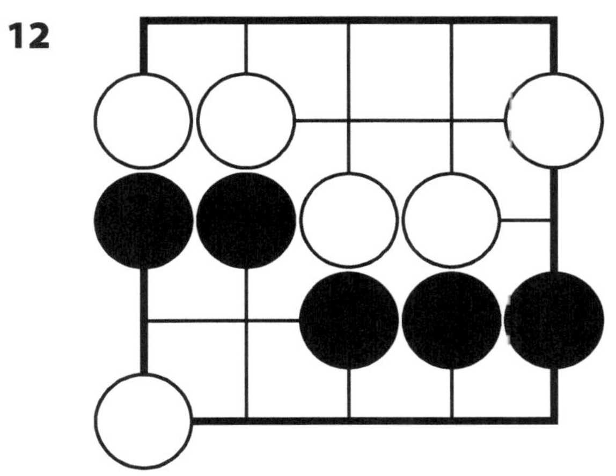

A grain of spice

Solution 11 Black wins by one point.

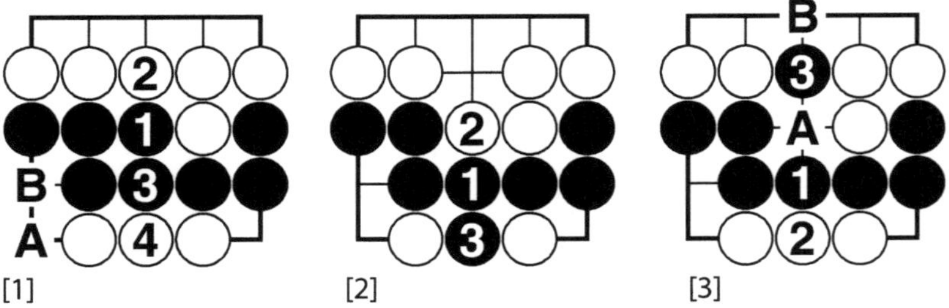

Dia. 1 (Failure) Trying to win with Black 1 does not work because White connects at 2. The game ends with Black 3 and White 4. Black A and White B create a ko, but Black has no ko threat. So, making a seki is best.

Dia. 2 (Correct) Black 1 is a calm move and the correct one. Even if White takes the center point with 2, Black 3 protects the territory. This way, Black wins by one point.

Dia. 3 (Variation) If Black 1 is answered by White 2, White will be punished by Black's wedge at 3. Then, A and B are miai.

Solution 12 Black wins by one point.

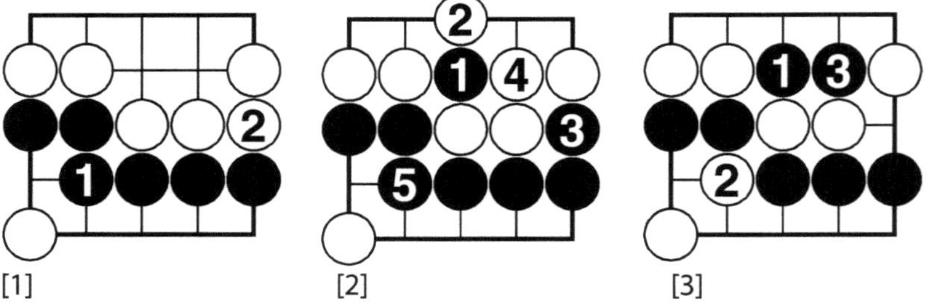

Dia. 1 (Failure) Black's connection at 1 seems unavoidable, but the game ends when White plays 2. The result is jigo, a failure for Black.

Dia. 2 (Correct) Black's cut at 1 is a clever move. If White answers at 2, Black 3 forces White to answer at 4, and Black finally defends with 5. If White plays 2 at 4, then connecting at 5 is the correct answer for Black. White still needs another defensive move.

Dia. 3 (Variation) If White answers with the cut at 2, Black counters with 3.

13

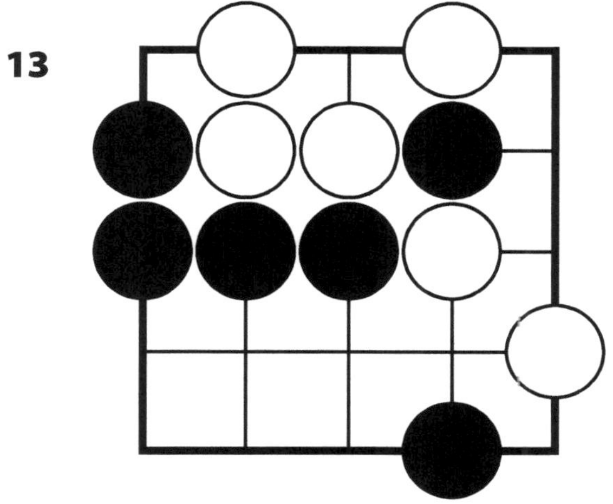

A matter of shape

14

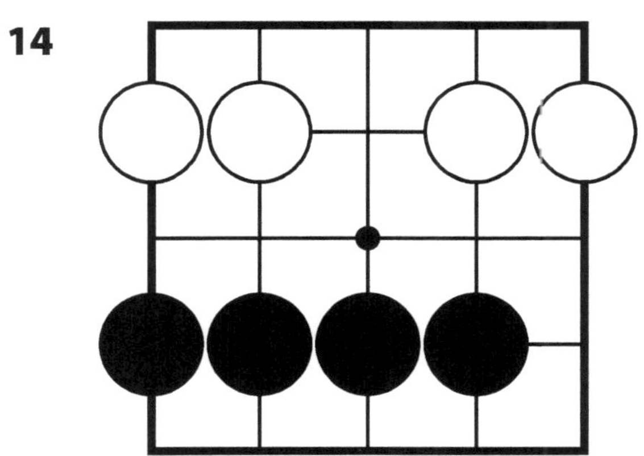

Points are full of...

Solution 13 Black wins by one point.

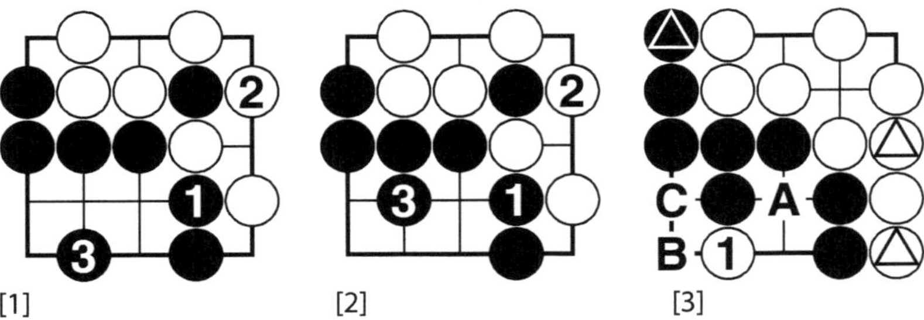

[1] [2] [3]

Dia. 1 (Correct) The first move to play is Black 1. White captures with 2. Then, the correct continuation for Black is defending at 3. Thus Black wins by one point.

Dia. 2 (Failure) Defending with Black 3 here is not a good strategy. Another defensive move will still be needed later on. This is a failure.

Dia. 3 (Continuation) When all neutral points are occupied, White takes the weak point of Black's shape. If now Black plays A, White kills at B. If Black plays B, White starts a ko at C, but Black doesn't have a single ko threat.

Solution 14 Black wins by one point.

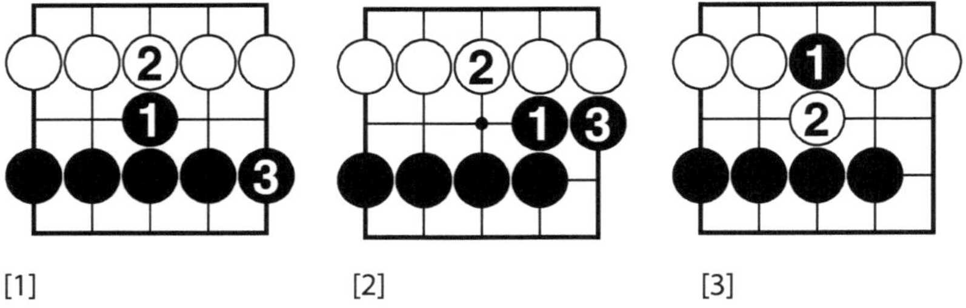

[1] [2] [3]

Dia. 1 (Failure) The sequence Black 1 to 3 is clearly a failure as the game ends in jigo. The question is, whether there is a way to expand Black's territory.

Dia. 2 (Correct) Black must attach at 1. This is the only move to win by one point. White defends at 2, and the game ends with Black 3. If White plays 2 at 3, Black will win with 3 at 2.

Dia. 3 (Failure) It is impossible to advance to Black 1 because White counters at 2. Black cannot win.

15

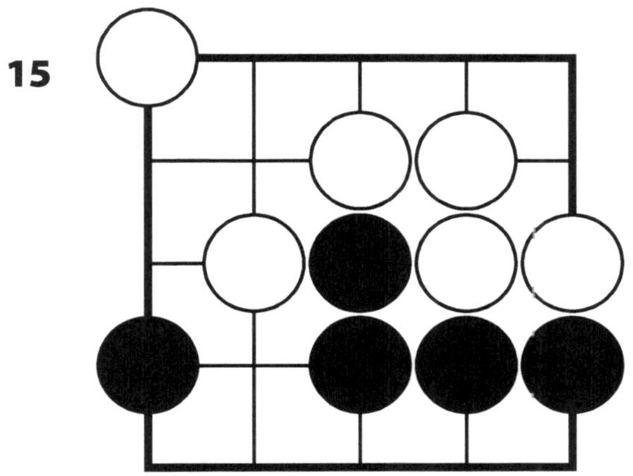

Sharp and powerful

16

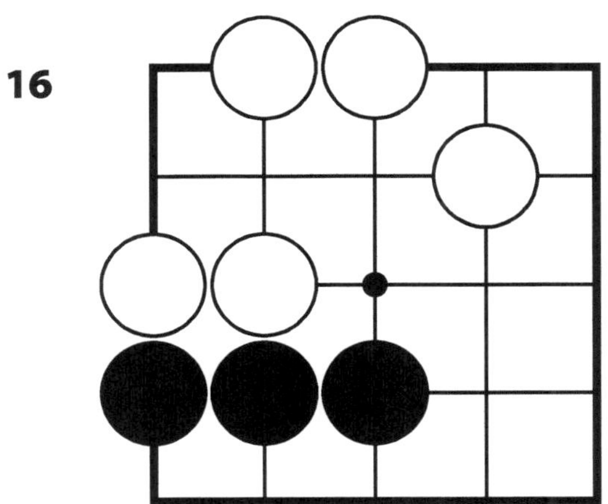

Start with the vital points

Solution 15　　Black wins by three points.

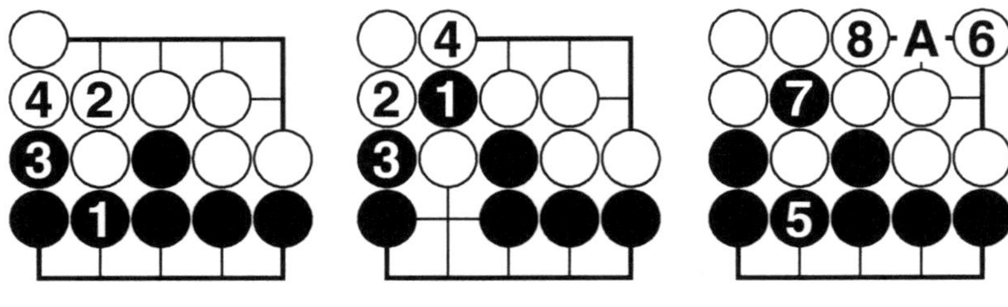

[1]　　[2]　　[3] *Black 9 below 7*

Dia. 1 (Failure) Black 1 is answered by White's connection at 2. The game ends with Black's push at 3 and White 4. The result is jigo, a failure.

Dia. 2 (Correct) Cutting with Black 1 is the correct move. If White plays 2, Black can advance to 3. White 4 captures a stone.

Dia. 3 (Continuation) After Black 5, White must make eyes at 6. Now Black can take a stone with 7. White is forced to connect at 8, and Black connects with 9 below 7. The result is a win by three points for Black. If White plays 6 at 7, Black will occupy at the vital point A.

Solution 16　　Black wins by one point.

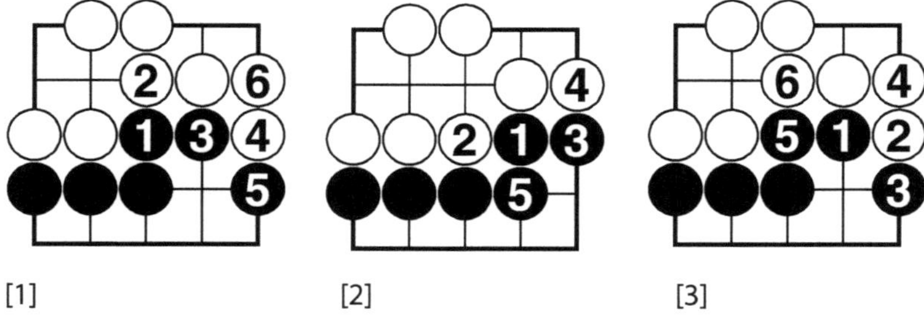

[1]　　[2]　　[3]

Dia. 1 (Correct) Black 1 and 3 are the correct endgame moves. Then the game ends with White 4, Black 5 and White 6. Black wins by one point. In this shape, point 1 is critical.

Dia. 2 (Failure) If Black plays 1, White will occupy the critical point at 2. After Black's connection at 5, the game ends in jigo. Black 3 at 5 is even worse. White then plays 3 and Black loses by one point.

Dia. 3 (Variation) White 2 is a mistake, as up to White 6 it leads to the same result as in the correct answer.

17

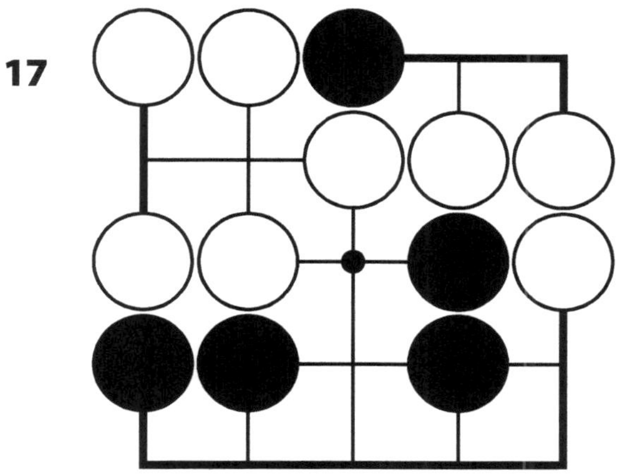

Sente, sente!

18

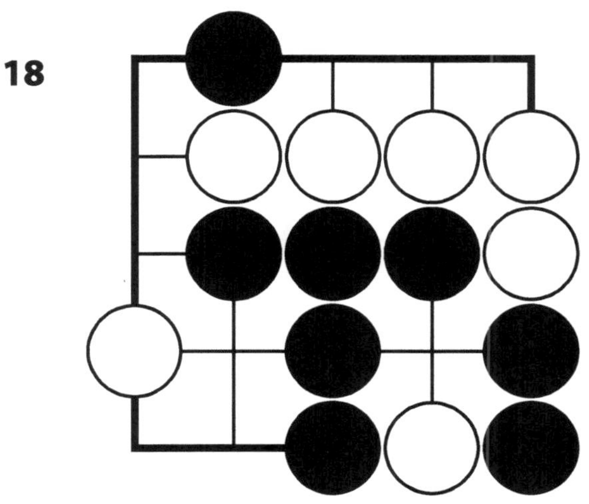

Be humble at times

Solution 17 **Black wins by one point.**

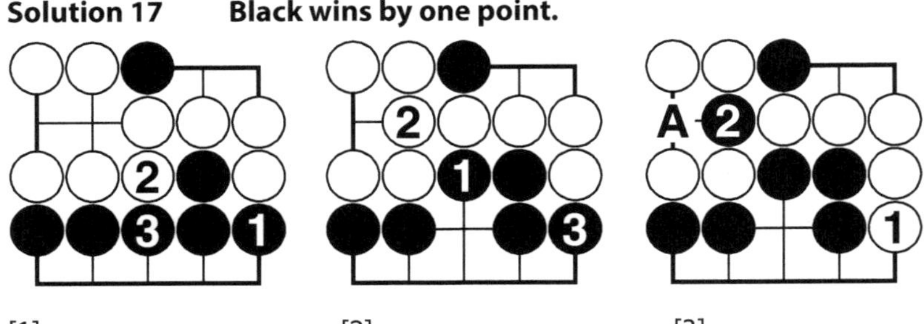

Dia. 1 (Failure) If Black plays 1 first, the game ends with White 2 and Black 3. Black fails, losing by one point.

Dia. 2 (Correct) Black 1 takes the critical point. White must answer at 2, then Black finishes the game with 3. Compared to the previous diagram, White's area has decreased by one point while Black's area has increased by one. Black wins by one point.

Dia. 3 (Variation) If White omits 2 in the previous diagram, Black will destroy White. White's capture at A fails, as this is a snapback.

Solution 18 **Black wins by one point.**

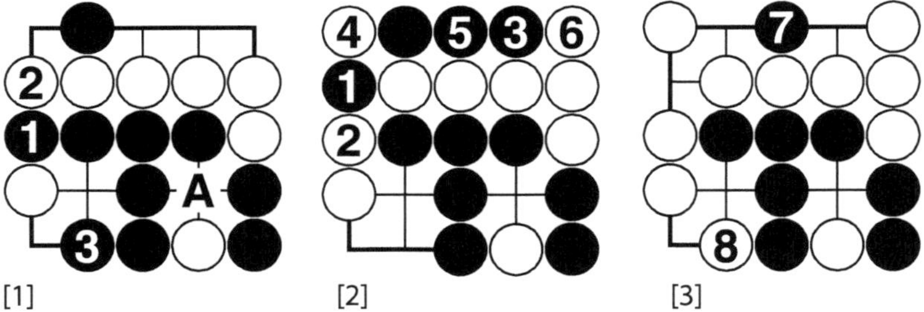

Dia. 1 (Correct) Black 1 will be answered by White 2. Then Black takes the critical point at 3. It's good to be humble at times. If White captures two stones at A, Black will capture White with a snapback playing the throw-in one point to the right of A.

Dia. 2 (Failure) It is not possible to launch a strong attack with Black 1. Even if Black tries, White will cut at 2. Up to White 6, Black loses four stones.

Dia. 3 (Continuation) Next, when Black 7 tries to kill, White counters with 8. Black is dead.

19

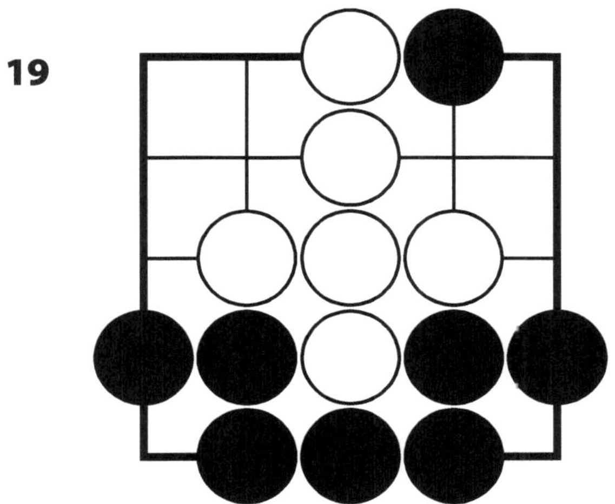

Consider White's response

20

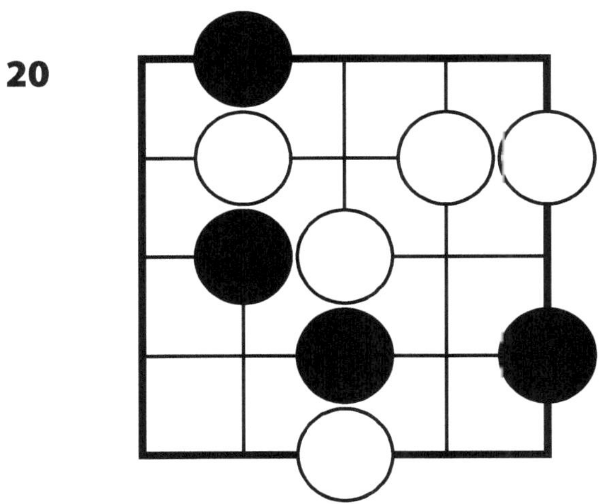

Get three moves right

Solution 19 Black wins by one point.

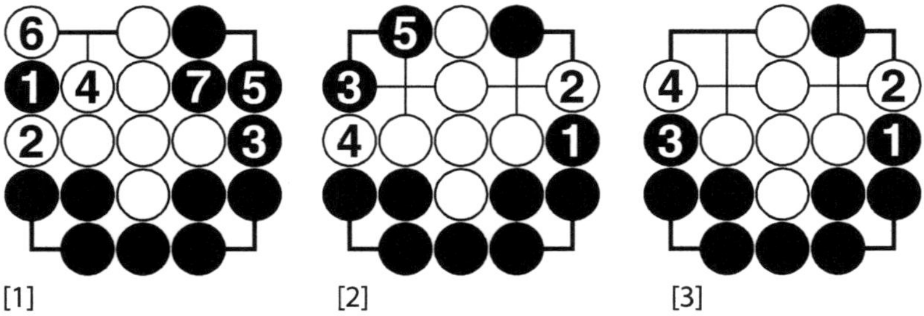

[1] [2] [3]

Dia. 1 (Failure) It's a mistake to play Black 1 and 3. White will respond with 4 and live at 6. After Black 7, each side has three points. If White plays 4 at 5, Black will create a seki with 5 at the point to the right of 6.

Dia. 2 (Correct) The correct sequence is Black 1 first, then continue with Black 3 and 5 to create a seki. White may capture one black stone, but this a single point only. Black has two points and wins by one.

Dia. 3 (Failure) Black 3 is clearly a failure.

Solution 20 Black wins by one point.

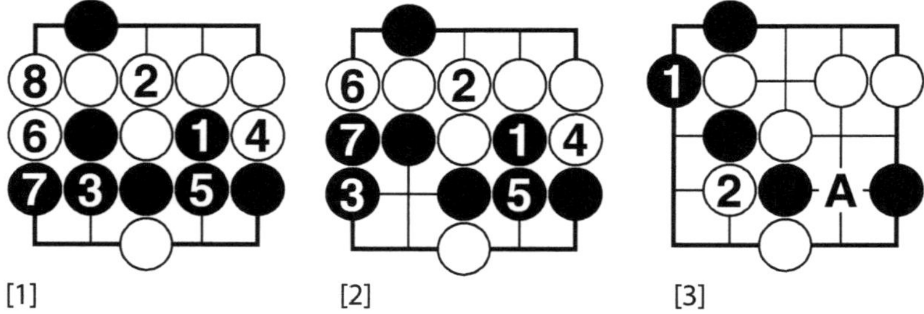

[1] [2] [3]

Dia. 1 (Failure) Black's atari at 1 and then connecting at 3, seems to be a natural way to play, but this is a mistake. After White 4 to 8, each side has six points. Jigo is a failure for Black.

Dia. 2 (Correct) After Black's atari at 1, the hanging connection is the correct continuation. In this position, White can only extend to 6. Next, Black plays 7 and wins by one point.

Dia. 3 (Failure) Black's atari at 1 is countered by White 2. Black loses. If Black plays 1 at 2, White simply answers at A.

21

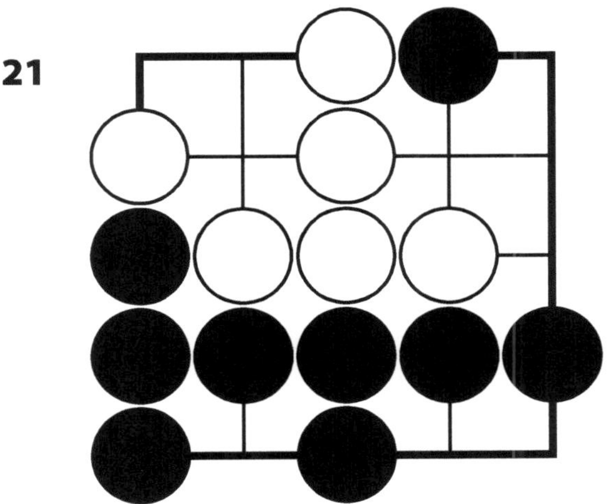

Inside out

22

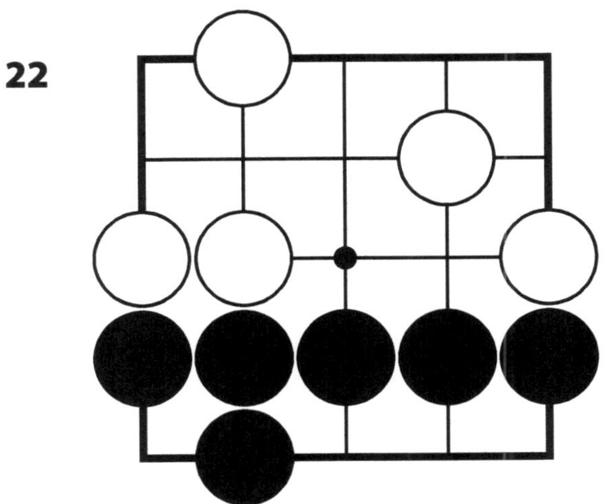

Looks like tesuji...

Solution 21 Black wins by one point.

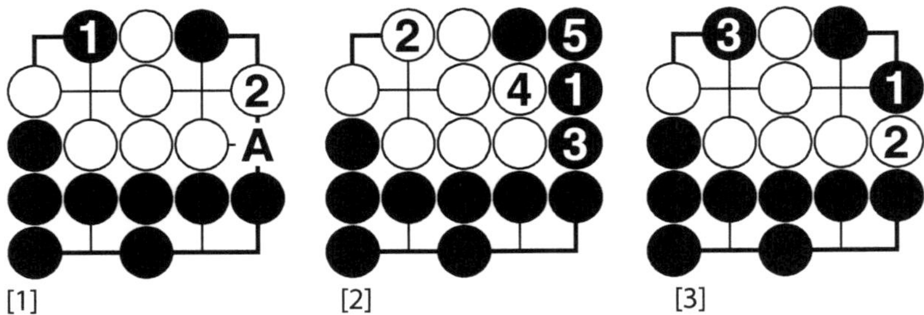

[1] [2] [3]

Dia. 1 (Failure) Black 1 takes one of the vital points, but White's kosumi at 2 is a good move. As it is, White has eight points and Black only three. White 2 at A would be a mistake, as Black answers at 2 and creates a seki. In this variation, White can capture a stone, but still Black wins by two points.

Dia. 2 (Correct) Black's kosumi at 1 is correct. White must make life with 2. Black wins by one point.

Dia. 3 (Variation) When White blocks at 2, Black 3 wins by creating a seki. White gains a point by capturing Black 3. Still, Black wins by two points.

Solution 22 Black wins by one point.

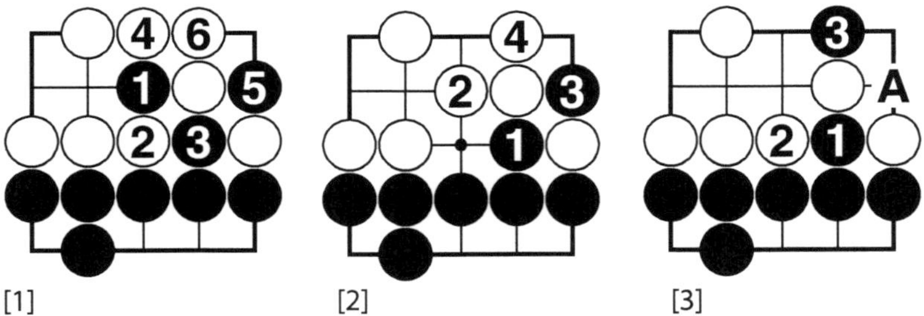

[1] [2] [3]

Dia. 1 (Failure) Black 1 seems to be a tesuji, but it fails. White defends with 2 and 4. When Black captures a stone with 5, White simply connects at 6. Each side has five points, a jigo position.

Dia. 2 (Correct) The correct move is Black 1. White draws back at 2, and Black captures a stone with 3. After White 4, Black wins by one point.

Dia. 3 (Variation) If White answers Black 1 with 2, Black can attack the shape with 3. Black 3 at A would be a mistake, as it will turn the game into jigo again.

23

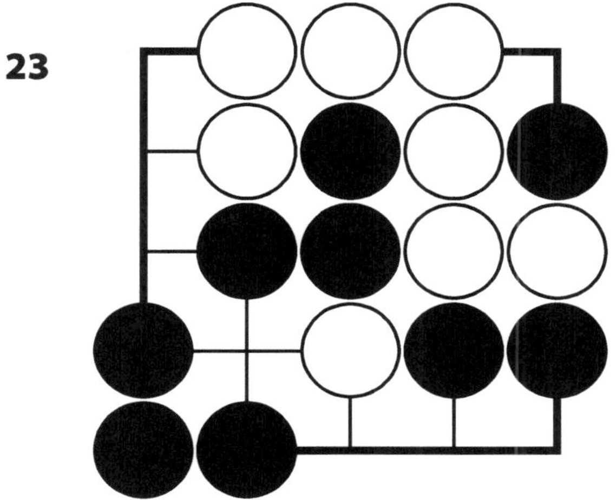

Take care, compare...

24

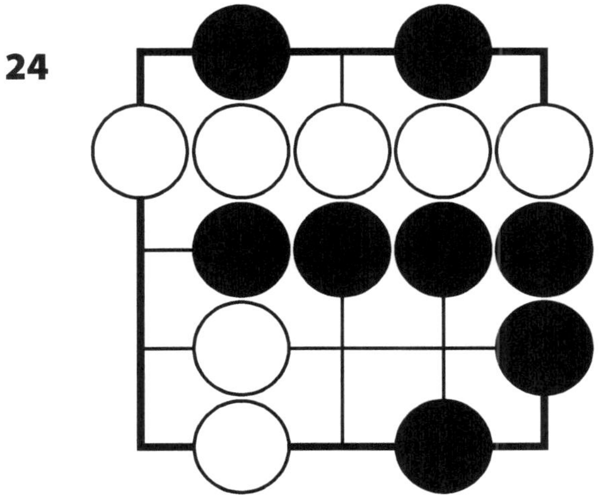

Beware of seki

Solution 23 Black wins by one point.

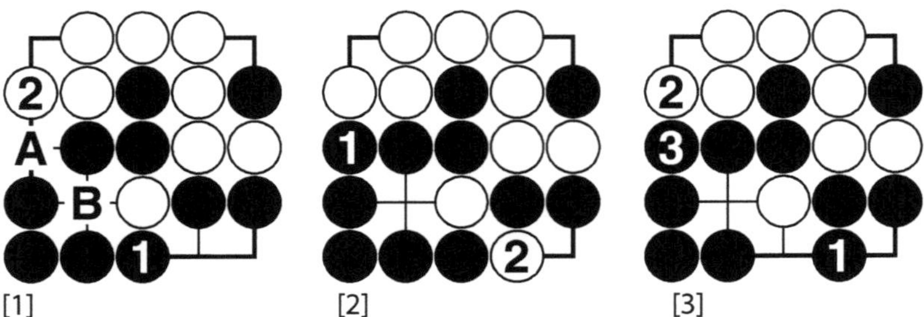

Dia. 1 (Failure) Black must take control of the white stone, but Black 1 is a failure. After White makes an eye at 2, Black cannot play A. Black even has to defend at B, when White approaches at A.

Dia. 2 (Reference) There is no way to play Black 1. White answers with 2, creating a double snapback.

Dia. 3 (Correct) The correct shape is Black 1. After White 2, Black can play 3, and wins by one point.

Solution 24 Black wins by one point.

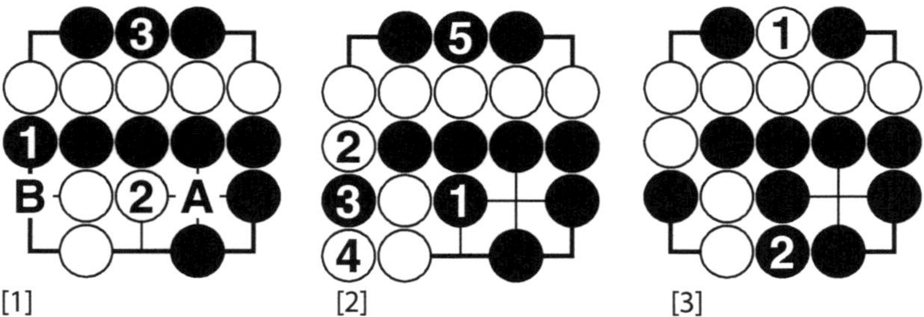

Dia. 1 (Failure) Black is tempted to block at 1, but this leaves behind a weak point. White 2 punishes the mistake by creating a seki. If Black now plays A, White takes B. If Black B, then White A. After Black 3, the whole board is a seki. Ending in jigo is a failure.

Dia. 2 (Correct) Black 1 securing the eye shape is the correct move. If White plays 2, Black will throw in at 3. After Black 5, there is a seki at the top while Black lives with points. Thus Black wins by one point.

Dia. 3 (Variation) If White, instead of 4 in the previous diagram, makes life with 1, Black captures with 2. This as well results in a win for Black.

25

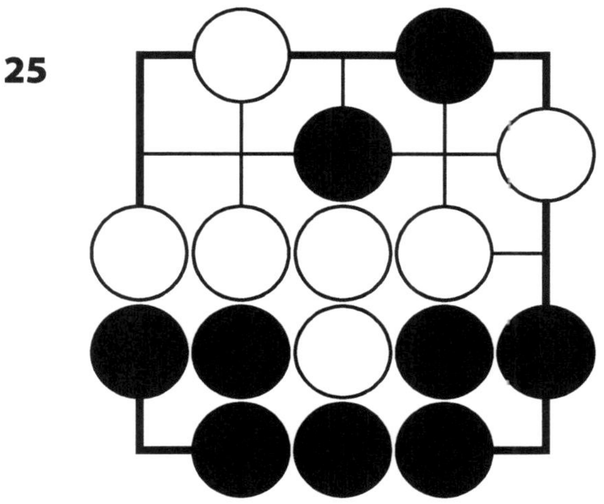

Even a seki wins

26

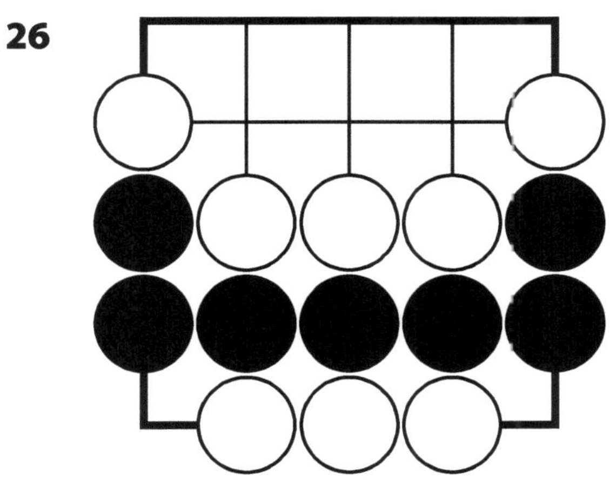

There is no black territory

Solution 25 Black wins by two points.

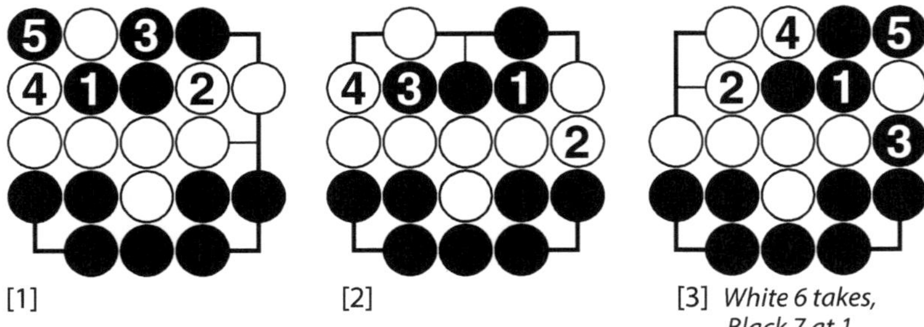

[1] [2] [3] *White 6 takes, Black 7 at 1*

Dia. 1 (Failure) The question is whether or not there is a move within White's area. Black 1 fails due to White 2. Black 3 and 5 create a ko, but Black has no ko threat. In the end, White wins the ko and Black loses the game.

Dia. 2 (Correct) Black 1 is a clever move. White connects at 2. After Black 3 and White 4, Black wins by two points.

Dia. 3 (Variation) The sequence White 2 to Black 5 creates an "under the stones" position. After White 6 takes, Black plays 7 at 1, and White can start a ko. But there is no ko threat, so White cannot win.

Solution 26 Black wins by one point.

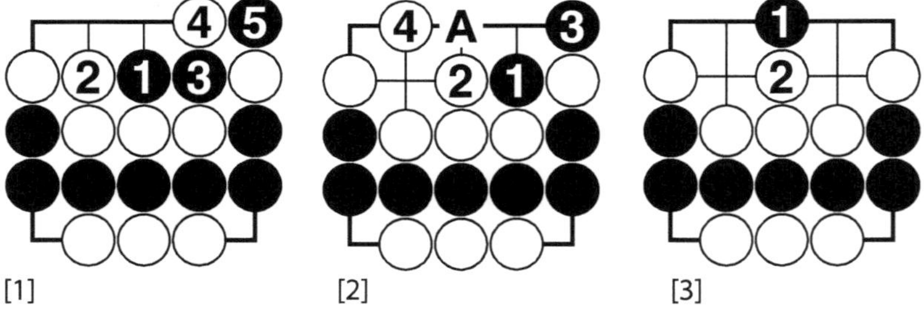

[1] [2] [3]

Dia. 1 (Correct) In symmetry, it is a good idea to play in the center like Black 1. If White connects at 2, Black cuts at 3. White 4 and Black 5 start a ko, but White has no ko threat. White cannot win.

Dia. 2 (Failure) Cutting on one side with Black 1 is a mistake. White will now live with 2 and 4. Black has only one point, so Black loses. There is no ko threat, so Black cannot play the ko at A.

Dia. 3 (Failure) Black 1 is played in the center of symmetry as well, but this is a mistake. White counters at 2 and there is no follow up for Black.

27

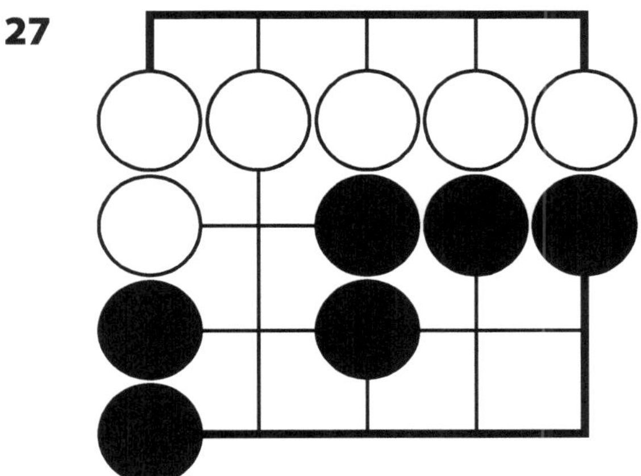

Advance or retreat?

28

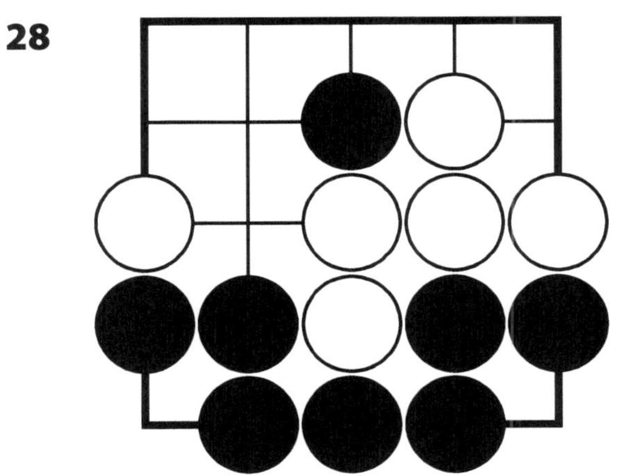

In endgame, from the outside...

Solution 27 Black wins by two points.

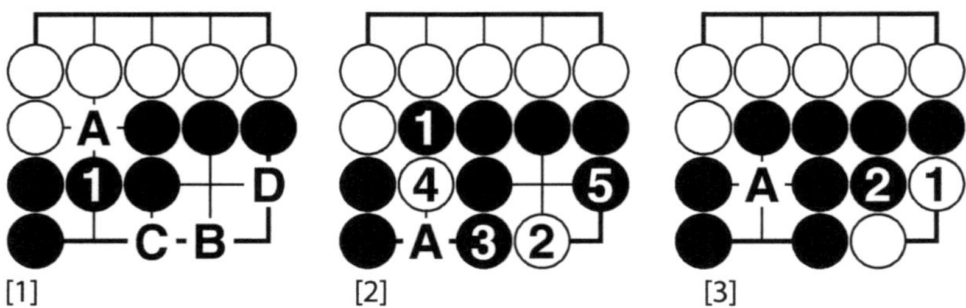

[1] [2] [3]

Dia. 1 (Failure) Retreating with Black 1 is a mistake. When the neutral point A is occupied, White can attack with B to D creating a seki. Hence, Black must defend at B or C. Now, each side has five points.

Dia. 2 (Correct) Black 1 is correct. When White now attacks at 2, Black defends with 3 and 5. Black wins by two points. If White captures two stones at A, Black will throw in one point to the left of 4.

Dia. 3 (Failure) If White plays 1 instead of 4 in the previous diagram, Black 2 leads to the same result. After White A, Black captures two white stones.

Solution 28 Black wins by two points.

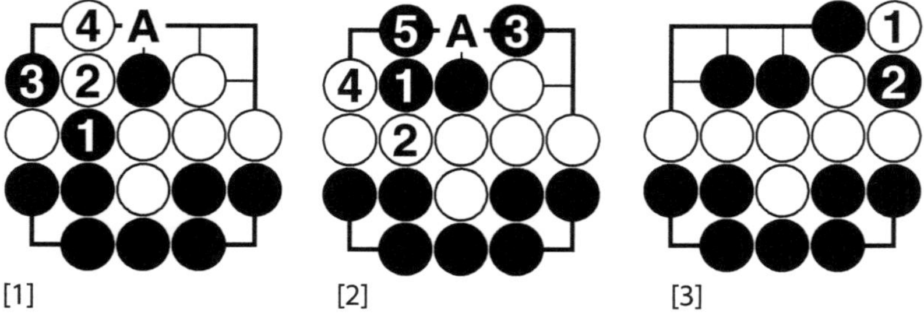

[1] [2] [3]

Dia. 1 (Failure) Black 1 is a common endgame move, but White defends with 2 and 4. The result is three points for Black, and five for White. White must capture at A later.

Dia. 2 (Correct) Here, Black can play 1. If White blocks the connection with 2, Black will continue at 3. After White 4 and Black 5 (or Black A), there is a ko in the upper right corner. Neither player can start the ko. The game is over, and Black wins by two points.

Dia. 3 (Variation) If, instead of 4 in the previous diagram, White starts a ko at 1 immediately, Black will take first. White has no ko threat and loses.

29

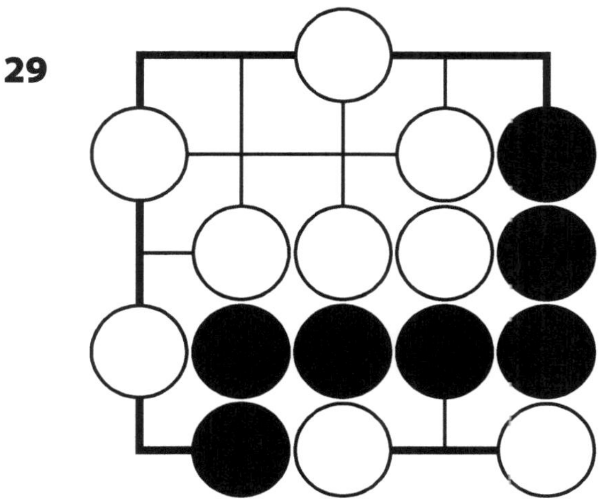

Superb tesuji

30

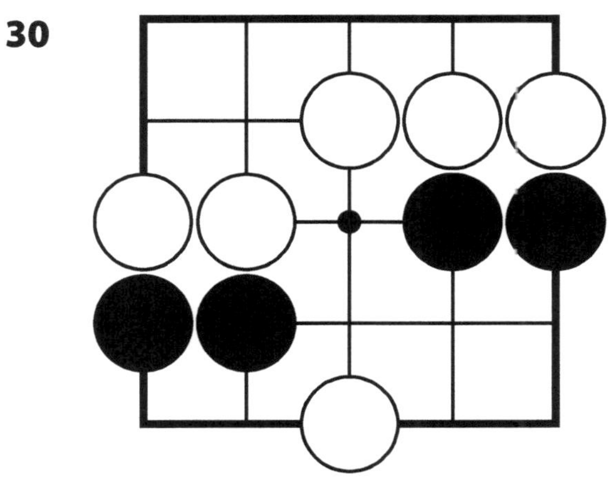

Taking care properly

Solution 29 **Black wins by one point.**

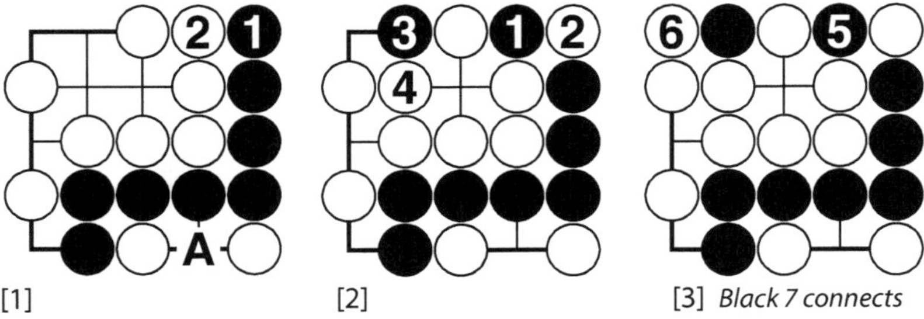

[1] [2] [3] *Black 7 connects*

Dia. 1 (Failure) It looks as if the game has ended already. After Black 1 and White 2, each side has four points of territory because Black still has to play A. This result is a failure for Black.

Dia. 2 (Correct) There is the superb tesuji of Black 1 to start a ko. White takes with 2, and Black plays the ko threat 3. White cannot connect at 1, but must defend with 4. Otherwise Black will kill with a move at 4.

Dia. 3 (Continuation) After Black takes the ko again with 5, there is not much for White to do except to capture at 6. After connecting the ko, Black wins by one point.

Solution 30 **Black wins by two points.**

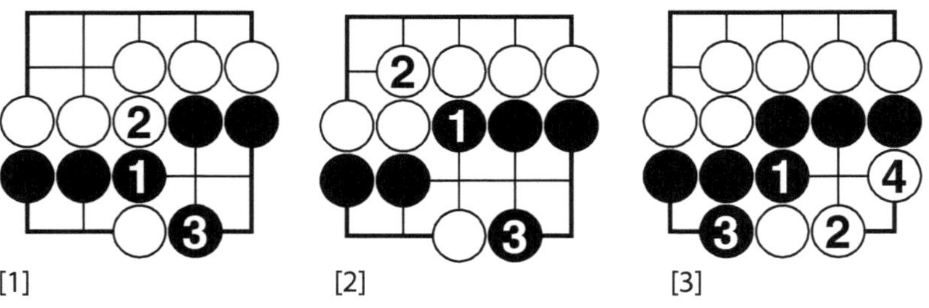

[1] [2] [3]

Dia. 1 (Failure) Playing safe with Black 1 is a bad idea. White 2 forces Black to defend at 3. The result is jigo, with each side having seven points.

Dia. 2 (Correct) Black must play 1 first. After White 2, Black 3 is the right answer. There is no further need to protect the territory. Thus Black wins by two points.

Dia. 3 (Failure) Black 1, instead of 3 in the previous diagram, is a bad move. White creates a seki with the sequence 2 to 4. Black loses.

31

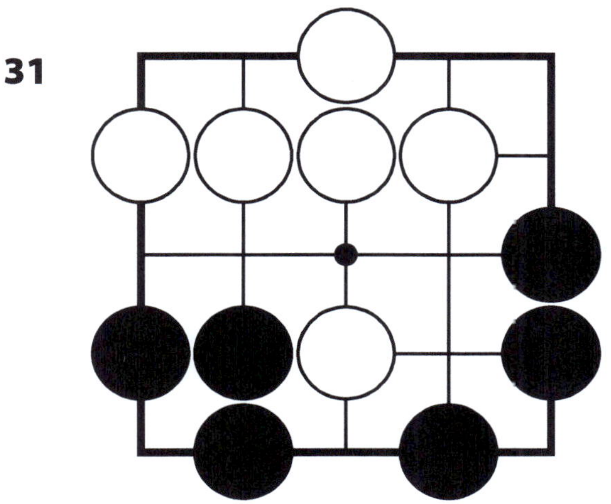

Let's see what you can do!

32

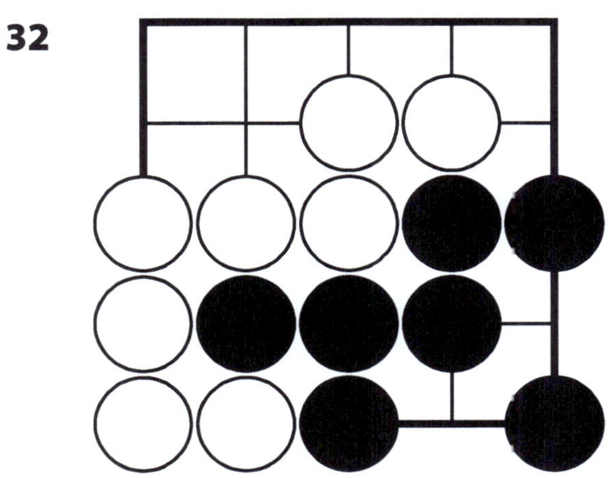

White's area is not enclosed yet

Solution 31 **Black wins by one point.**

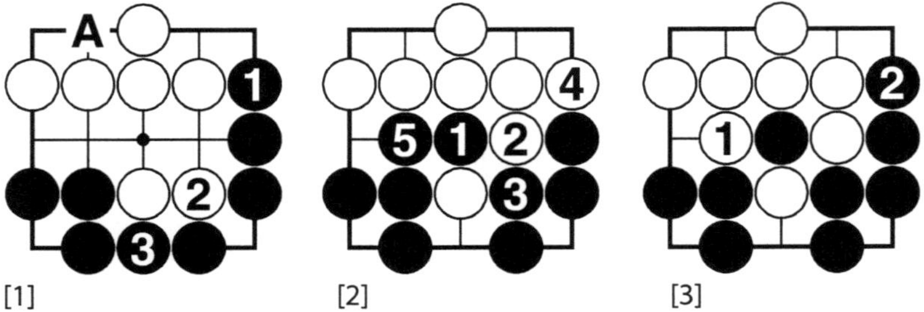

Dia. 1 (Failure) Black' s push at 1 is countered by White 2. In the end, Black has to throw in at A in order to prevent White from approaching. After A, the whole board position is seki, but Black loses by one point.

Dia. 2 (Correct) Black 1 is the tesuji. White 2 is natural. With 3, Black makes an eye in the corner. Next, White lives by making an eye with 4, and Black finishes the game with 5. Black wins by one point.

Dia. 3 (Variation) Instead of White 4 in the previous diagram, White may capture at 1, but White dies when Black pushes along the edge at 2.

Solution 32 **Black wins by two points.**

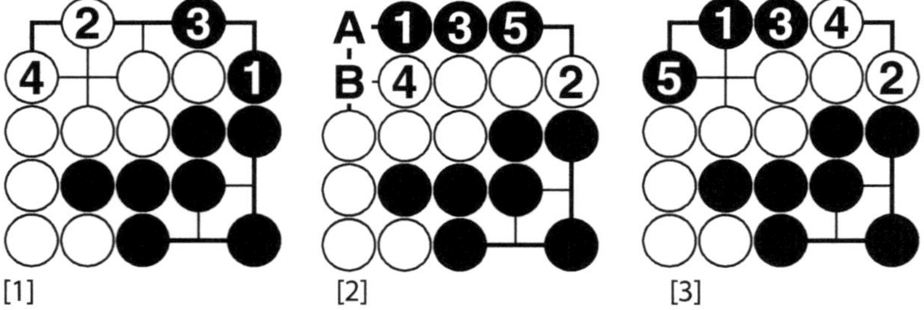

Dia. 1 (Failure) Black 1 is a standard endgame move. White makes life with 2 and 4. Both sides have two points, it's jigo. If Black 1 at 3 first, it is good enough for White to play 2. After Black 3 at 1 and White 4, the result is the same.

Dia. 2 (Correct) Black's placement at 1 occupies the vital point. Even if White extends to 2, Black 3 and 5 create a seki. Black wins by two points. White has no ko threat to play A and to allow Black B.

Dia. 3 (Variation) If White blocks at 4, Black creates a seki with 5.

33

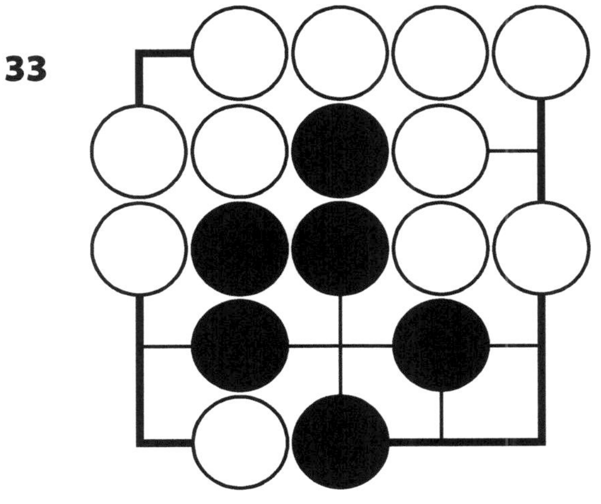

Which way?

34

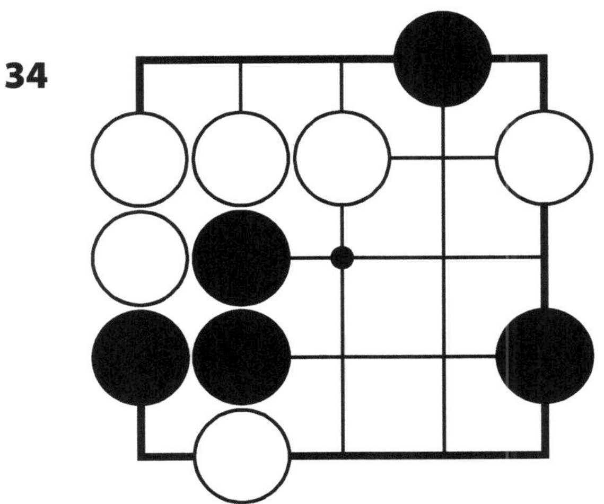

Three moves to read

Solution 33 Black wins by one point.

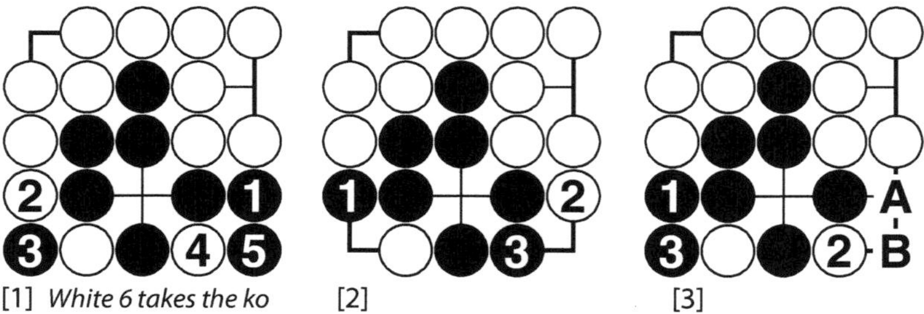

[1] *White 6 takes the ko* [2] [3]

Dia. 1 (Failure) Blocking with Black 1 is a mistake. After White 2 and Black 3, there is a ko. White has the ko threat 4, so Black must capture. Next, White takes the ko leaving Black no way to play. Black is completely destroyed.

Dia. 2 (Correct) Black 1 is the correct answer. After White 2, Black defends at 3. Finally capturing a stone, Black wins by one point.

Dia. 3 (Variation) When White plays 2, Black 3 is correct. Next, White A, Black B takes, White passes, and Black connects. Black 3 at B is a mistake because of White A and Black 3. Now, White takes the ko first at 2.

Solution 34 Black wins by one point.

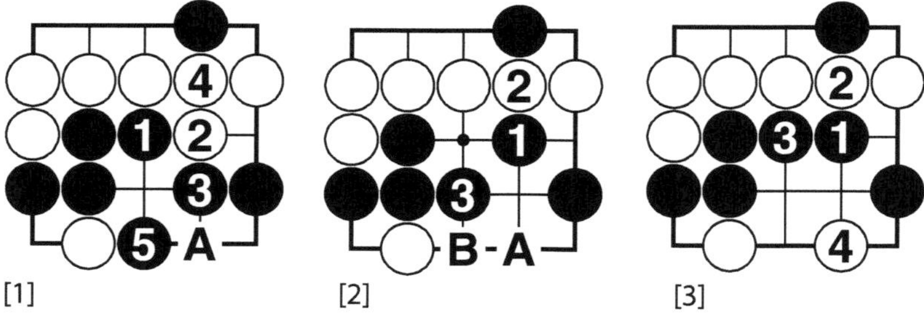

[1] [2] [3]

Dia. 1 (Failure) Expanding the territory with Black 1 is a mistake. White pushes at 2 and connects at 4. Black must now defend at 5. The result is jigo. If Black omits 5, White will be able to play A and Black loses.

Dia. 2 (Correct) Black must first play the kosumi at 1. Next, Black 3 is an important move. Black wins by one point. White A will be answered with Black B.

Dia. 3 (Variation) It's greedy for Black to play 3. White will punish this move with 4. There is no way out for Black, as the bottom area turned into a seki.

35

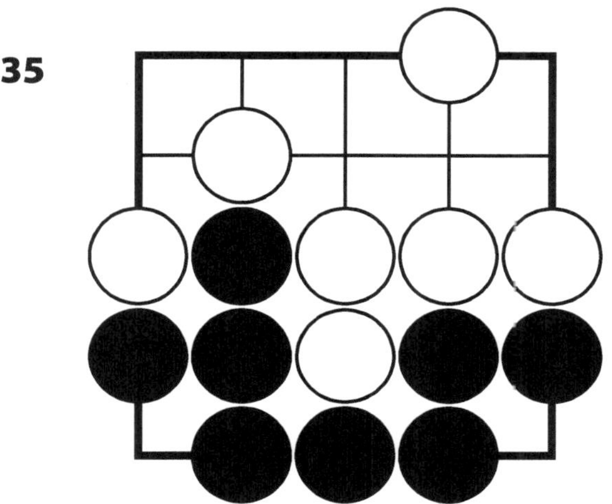

Corner tesuji

36

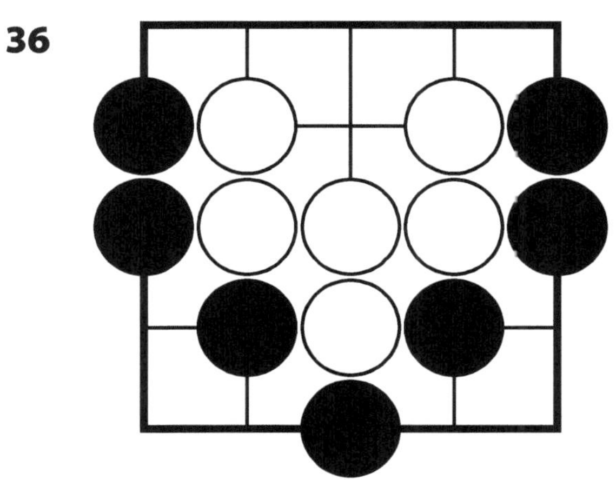

Is the saying true?

Solution 35 Black wins by one point.

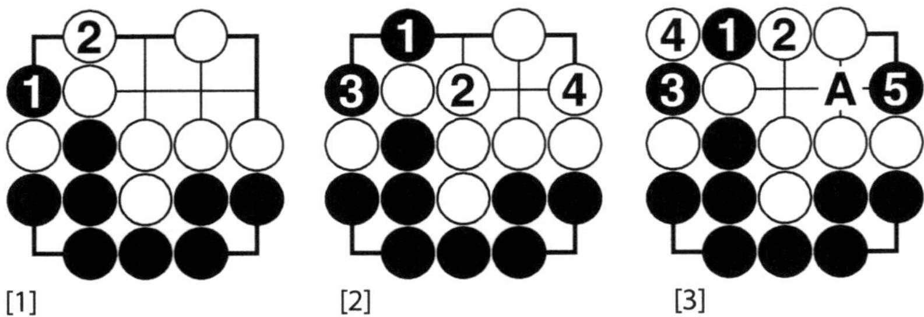

Dia. 1 (Failure) If Black simply captures a stone with 1, the game ends with White extending to 2. Black loses by two points.

Dia. 2 (Correct) Black's clamp at 1 is the correct move. When White draws back at 2, Black 3 can advance one step. White must live with 4, and thus Black wins by one point.

Dia. 3 (Variation) It's a strong counter to play White 2. After White 4, there is a ko. However, White is forced to answer Black's threat at A. Black retakes the ko at 1, and there is no way for White to win.

Solution 36 Black wins by two points.

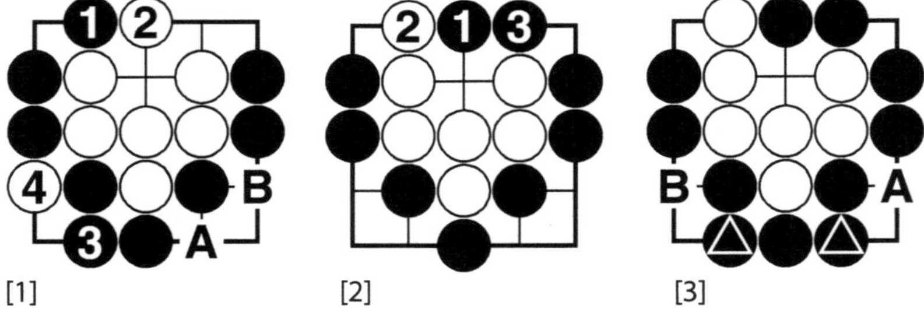

Dia. 1 (Failure) If Black plays 1, White makes an eye at 2, and no matter how the rest is played, it will be "one eye against no eye". Black will be annihilated.

Dia. 2 (Correct) Black 1 goes with the saying "In a symmetrical shape, play in the center!" and is the correct answer. White 2 and Black 3 are miai. There is no other move for either side, the whole board is a seki.

Dia. 3 (Continuation) In this shape, when Black plays the marked stones, White has to throw in twice to keep the status of seki. Hence Black wins by two points gained from capturing two white stones.

37

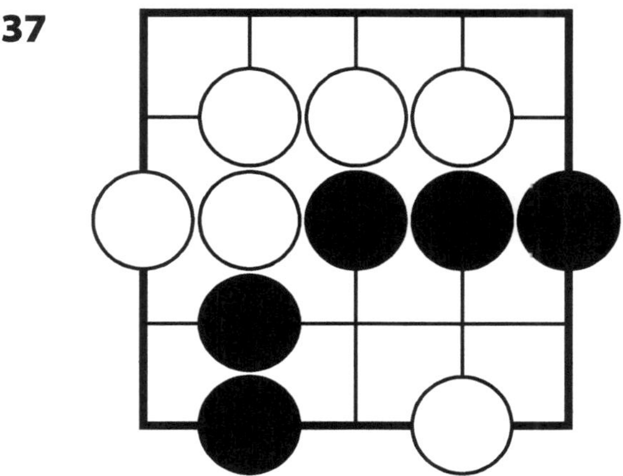

The key point

38

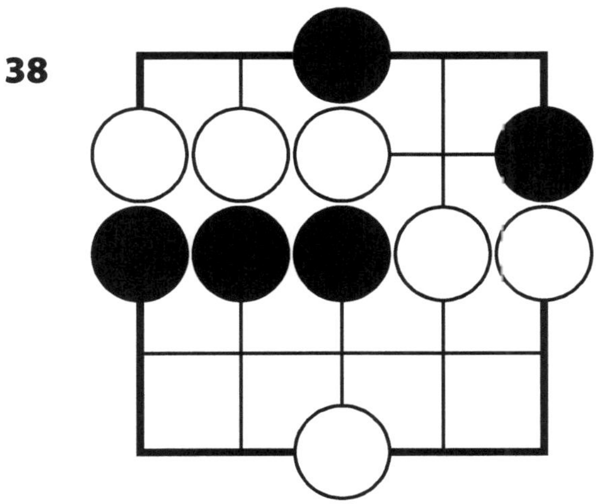

The use of discarded stones

Solution 37 **Black wins by one point.**

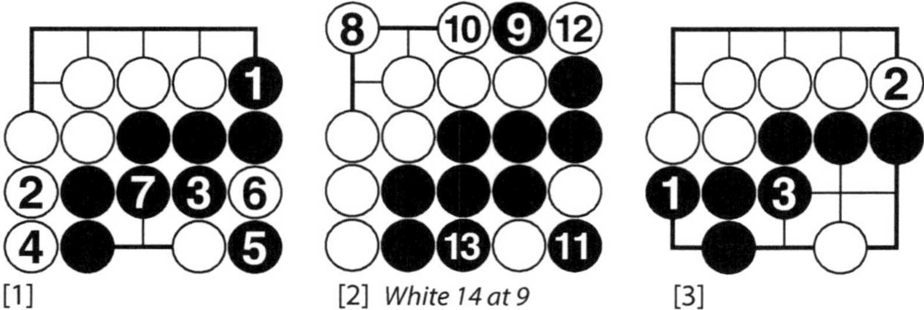

[1] [2] *White 14 at 9* [3]

Dia. 1 (Failure) Black 1 is a strong move to aim at White's eye shape, but it does not work. If White counter attacks with 2, Black must defend at 3. Then White 4 to 6 start a ko. Black has no choice but to connect at 7.

Dia. 2 (Continuation) Next, White makes life with 8. After the sequence Black 9 to White 14, the game results in jigo.

Dia. 3 (Correct) The correct answer is making a second eye with Black 1. After White 2 and Black 3, the game ends with seven points for Black. Black wins by one point. Very simple.

Solution 38 **Black wins by one point.**

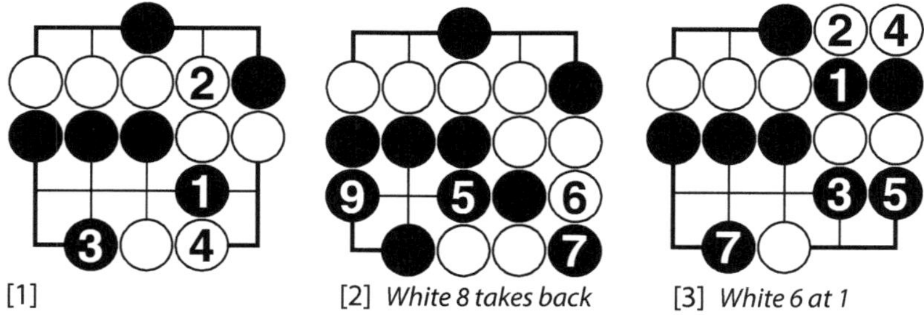

[1] [2] *White 8 takes back* [3] *White 6 at 1*

Dia. 1 (Failure) Black 1 is a poor attempt. White just connects at 2. If Black plays 3 now, White 4 is a clever response.

Dia. 2 (Continuation) Next, when Black takes the two stones with 5 and 7, White takes back one point to the left of 7. Black is alive with 9, but loses by a large margin.

Dia. 3 (Correct) Black 1 makes use of the discarded stone. Black 3 and 5 keep up the pressure. At the end, Black comes back to play 7. Black has eight points, one more than White.

39

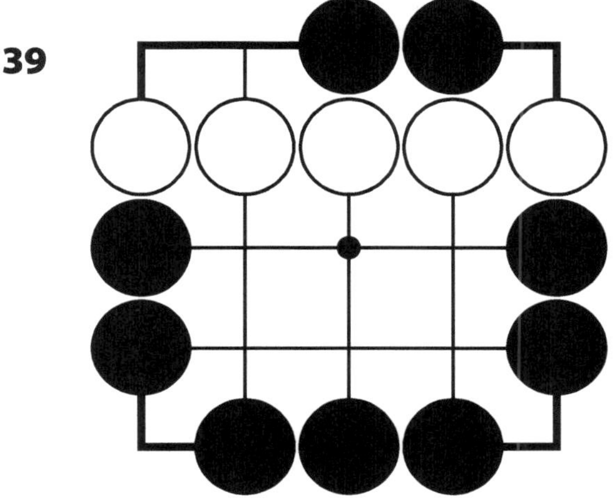

Count White's area

40

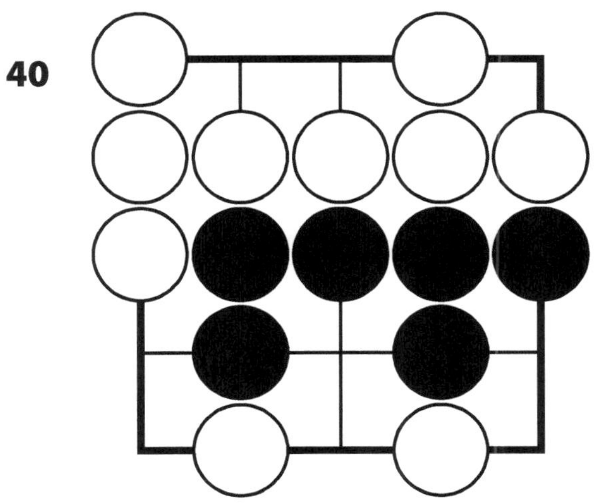

The crucial move is the first

Solution 39 Black wins by one point.

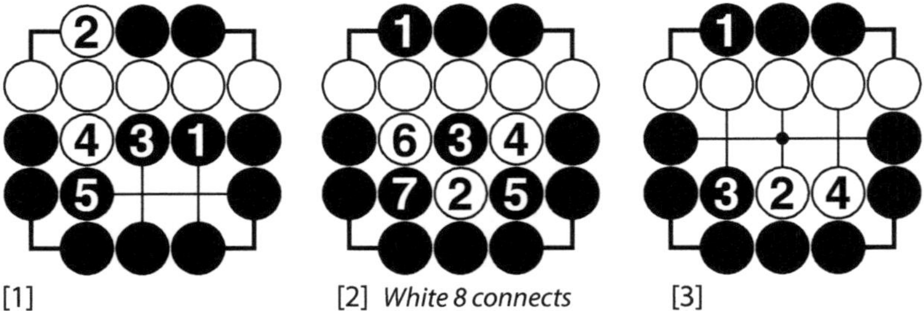

[1] [2] *White 8 connects* [3]

Dia. 1 (Failure) Enlarging Black's area at 1 is a mistake. Black cannot win by surrounding two points with three moves. White even has time to ensure life with 2, and then still to push at 4. Black loses by two points.

Dia. 2 (Correct) The correct answer is making a seki with Black 1. Black's wedge at 3 is the best way to deal with White 2. After White 4 to 8, Black wins by one point.

Dia. 3 (Variation) If Black plays 3 like this, White 4 is Black's death.

Solution 40 Black wins by one point.

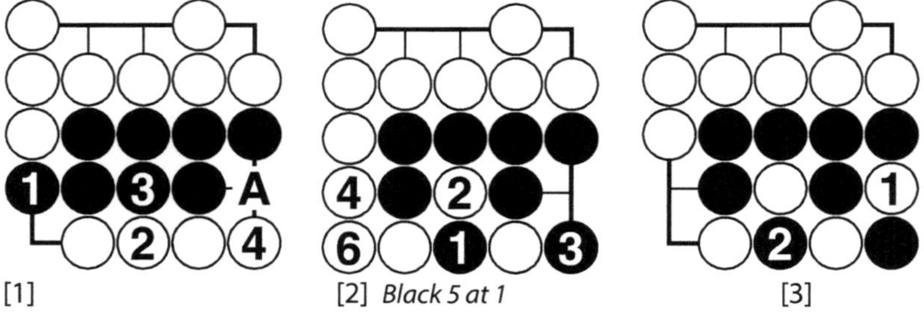

[1] [2] *Black 5 at 1* [3]

Dia. 1 (Failure) Black 1 is a mistake as White creates a seki with 2 and 4. Since White has three points, Black loses by three points. Black cannot start a ko with 3 at 4. There is no ko threat after White captures at A.

Dia. 2 (Correct) Black 1 and 3 are the tesuji combination. After White 4, Black 5 captures two stones. The game ends with the connection at 6, and Black wins by one point.

Dia. 3 (Variation) Instead of 4 in the previous diagram, White may consider the capture at 1, but Black plays 2. There are now two ko. When White takes one, Black takes the other. So Black wins.

Chapter 3: JUMP

Black to play and win!

1

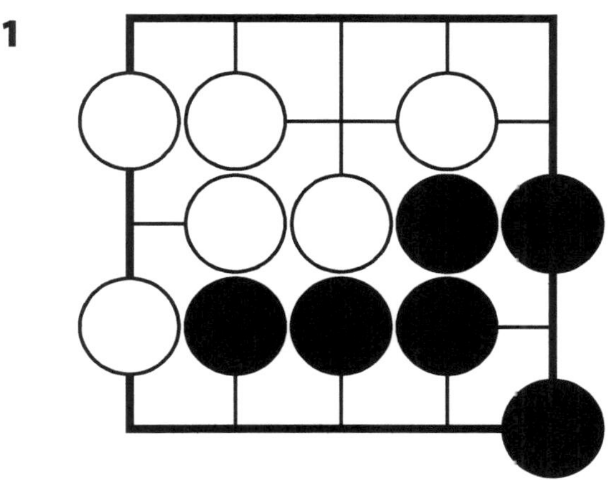

White's serious weakness

2

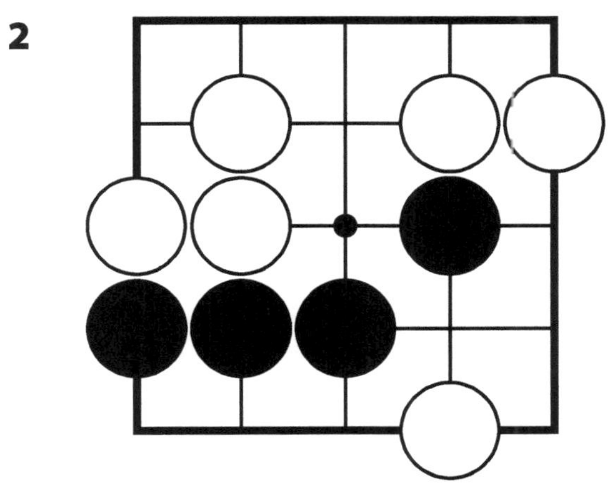

Get to the point

Solution 1 Black wins by three points.

[1]

[2] *White 10 passes, Black 11 at 6*

[3] *Black 7 at 1*

Dia. 1 (Failure) Black 1 will be answered by White 2 in the usual way. After the neutral points are taken, White must capture a stone at A. The result is jigo. More ingenuity is required of Black.

Dia. 2 (Correct) Black 1 hits the critical point. After White 2, Black 3 is decisive. The problem for White is the lack of ko threats, so White is forced to connect at 4. Black 5 creates a seki at the top edge. White cannot win the ko starting with Black 9. Black wins by three points.

Dia. 3 (Variation) After Black 1, White 2 is a strong move which starts a sequence that leads to a ko. Again, after Black 7, White has no ko threat.

Solution 2 Black wins by one point.

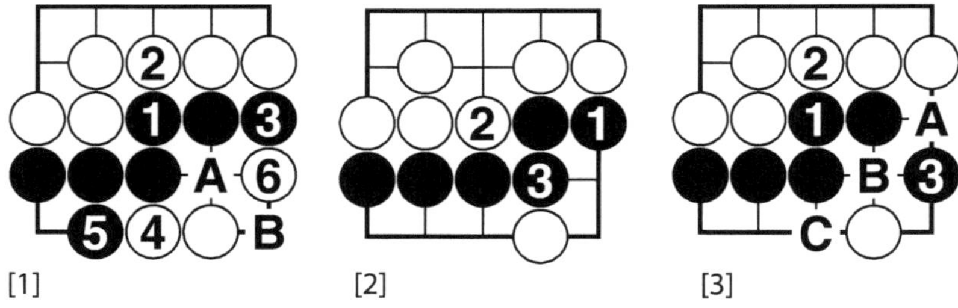

[1] [2] [3]

Dia. 1 (Failure) Black 1 is sente. After blocking at 3, White creates a seki taking all points. Black loses by six points. White must not play 4 at 6 as Black counters with A. Next White at 4, Black starts a ko at B and wins.

Dia. 2 (Failure) Simply playing Black 1 is a failure. White 2 forces Black to connect at 3. Each side has seven points, a failure for Black.

Dia. 3 (Correct) Black 3 is the correct way to continue. Black now has seven points while there are only six for White. Black wins by one point. Black must not respond to White A. When White attacks at B, Black defends in time at C.

3

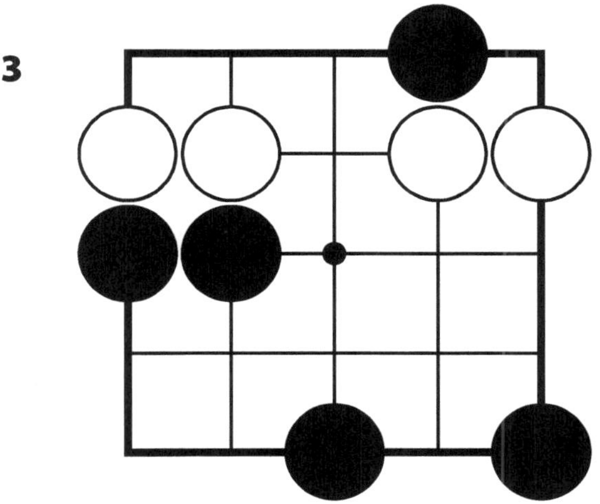

Be careful at the end

4

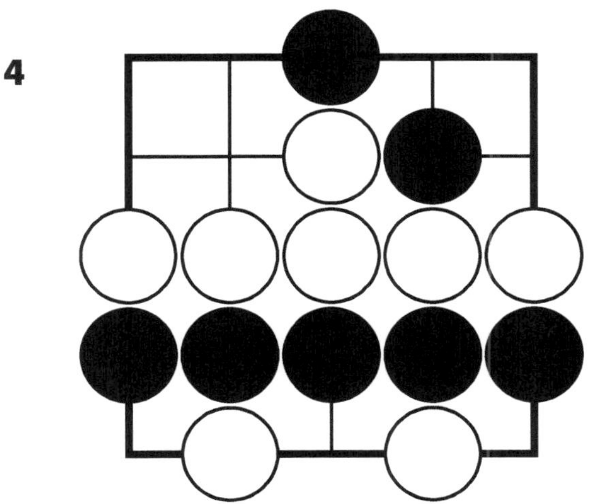

Without losing everything

Solution 3 **Black wins by one point.**

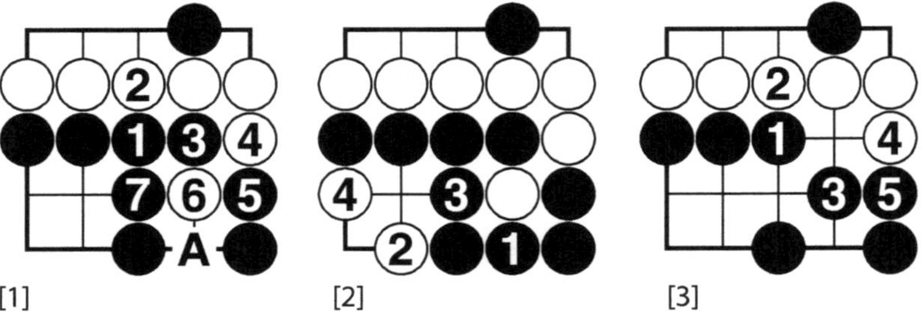

Dia. 1 (Correct) The correct answer is Black 1 and 3. When White pushes at 4, Black defends at 5. After White 6, Black secures the territory with 7. If White captures at A, Black plays the throw-in at 5 in return.

Dia. 2 (Variation) Defending with Black 1 is a mistake. White 2 and 4 create a seki and Black loses by five points.

Dia. 3 (Failure) Black 3 fails because after Black 5, the result is jigo.

Solution 4 **Black wins by one point.**

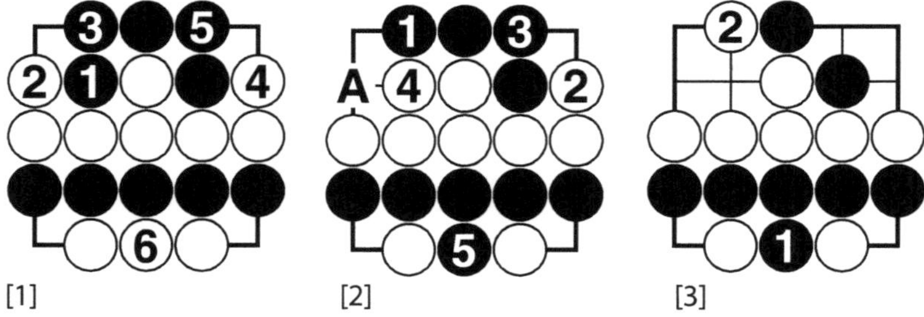

Dia. 1 (Failure) Black 1 seems to be a good move, but when White counters with 2 and 4, the upper side becomes seki. Next, White 6 creates a seki on the lower side too. Both players have zero points, jigo.

Dia. 2 (Correct) Black 1 is the correct move. White must play 2 and 4 to avoid being captured. So, Black comes back to make life and take territory. Black wins by six points.

Dia. 3 (Failure) If Black starts with 1, White counters at 2, and Black loses by four points.

5

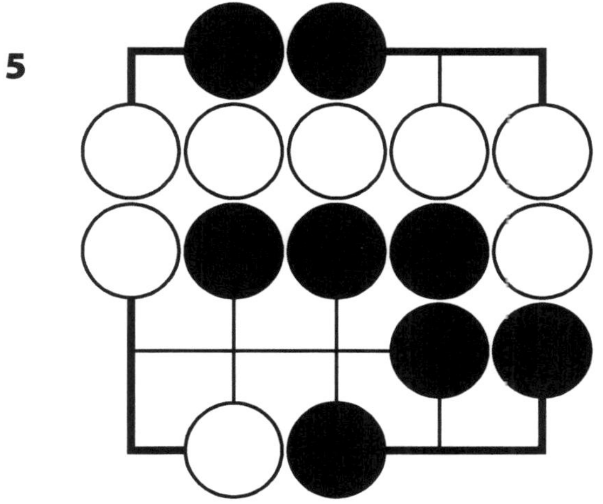

No room for complacency

6

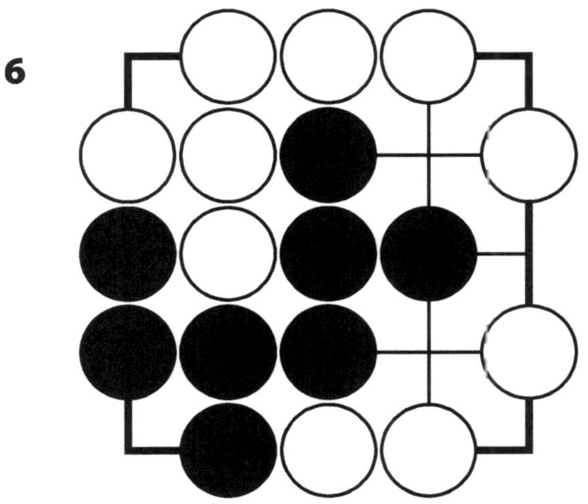

Removed stones do count

Solution 5 **Black wins by one point.**

[1] [2] [3]

Dia. 1 (Failure) It's not a good idea to play a game where you can't win. Black 1 is answered by White 2, and with Black 3 the game ends with six points each.

Dia. 2 (Correct) Black's block at 1 is correct. Black 3 is the correct response to White 2, and White 4 finishes the game. Black wins by one point.

Dia. 3 (Reference) Black 1 instead of 3 in the previous diagram is a mistake. White 2 kills as Black cannot approach the white stones. Black A looks like a seki, but White can still capture Black's stones at the bottom.

Solution 6 **Black wins by one point.**

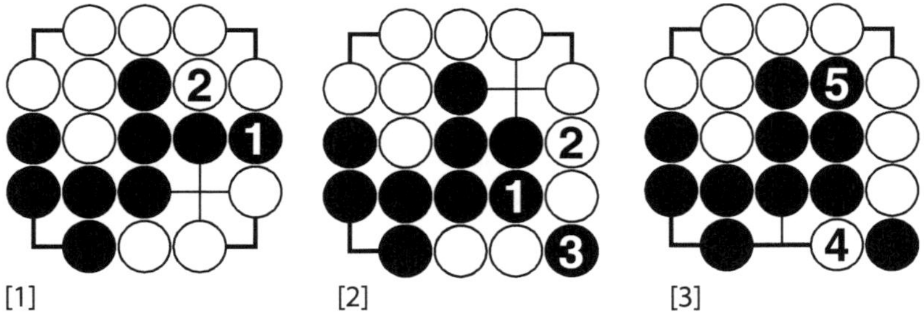

[1] [2] [3]

Dia. 1 (Failure) The normal block with Black 1 is answered by White 2, which makes life for the white stones. The lower side is now seki, so Black loses by two points.

Dia. 2 (Correct) The correct move is the tesuji of Black 1. When White connects at 2, Black 3 captures two stones.

Dia. 3 (Continuation) After Black 3, White 4 retakes a single stone in the corner. However, Black wins the game with 5, as Black has one more capture than White. The board position is seki, there are no points to count.

7

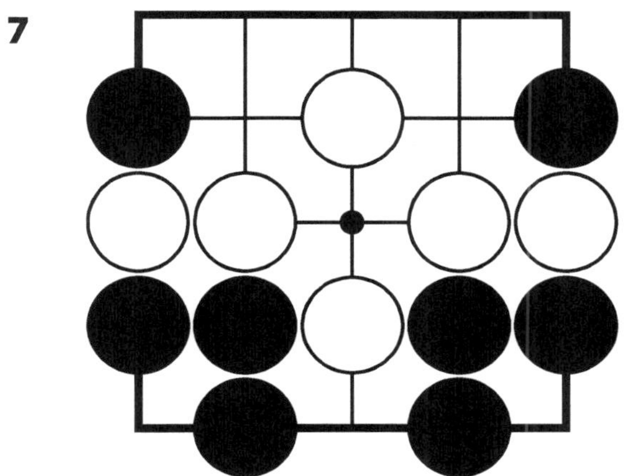

Be precise in your steps

8

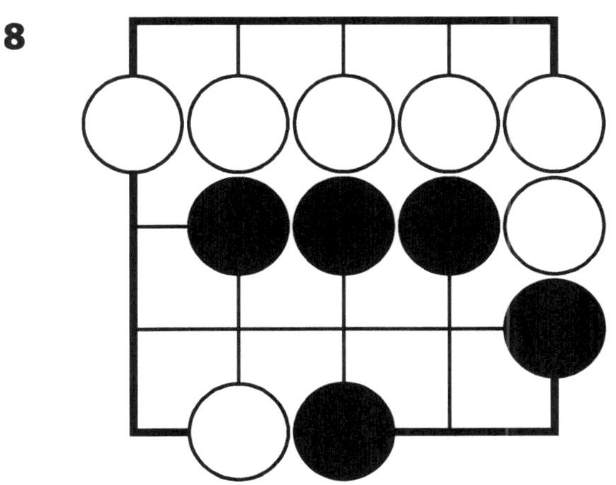

The depth of five lines

Solution 7 **Black wins by one point.**

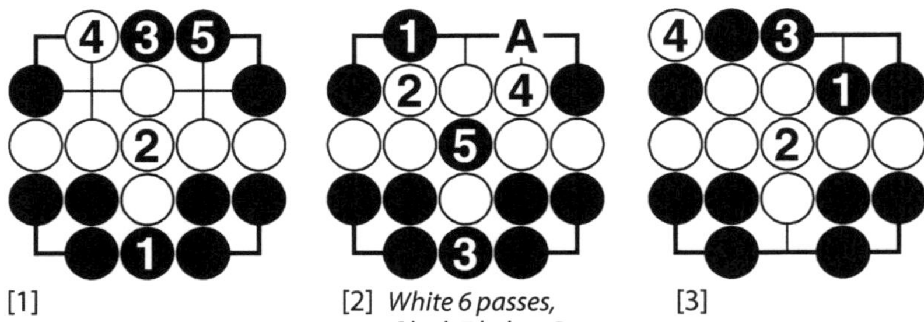

[1] [2] *White 6 passes, Black 7 below 5* [3]

Dia. 1 (Correct) After Black and White connecting at 1 and 2 respectively, Black 3 is a clever move. With White 4 and Black drawing back at 5, a seki has been created. White has only one stone captured in the upper left corner, so the result is a win for Black by one point.

Dia. 2 (Failure) Black's kosumi 1 is not a good move. After Black 5, the game ends with Black connecting the ko in the center. Even if Black plays A, White lives with a double ko, one in each corner. Black loses.

Dia. 3 (Failure) If Black 1 and 3, White 4 wins because there is no ko threat for Black. Black loses by one point.

Solution 8 **Black wins by two points.**

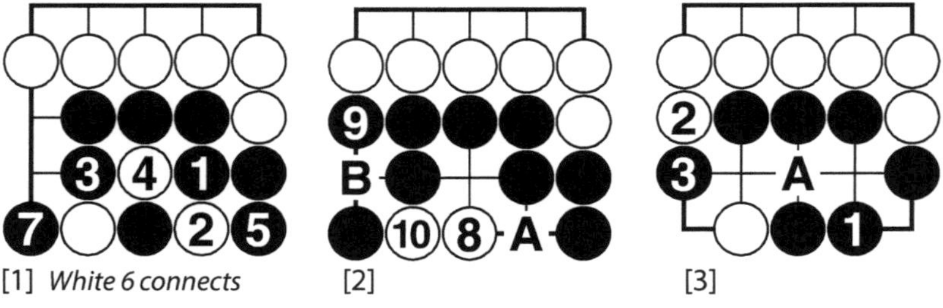

[1] *White 6 connects* [2] [3]

Dia. 1 (Failure) White will answer Black's connection at 1 with the strong move 2. Next, Black 5, White 6 connects, and Black 7 takes four stones.

Dia. 2 (Continuation) White 8 is a clever move. Even if Black plays at A after White 10, White starts a ko at B. Black has no ko threat and dies.

Dia. 3 (Correct) Black 1 hits the shape point. After White 2, the block at 3 is correct. Black wins by two points. If Black plays A instead of 1, White will answer at 3. Next Black 2, and finally White 1. The result would be a seki, and Black would lose by four points.

9

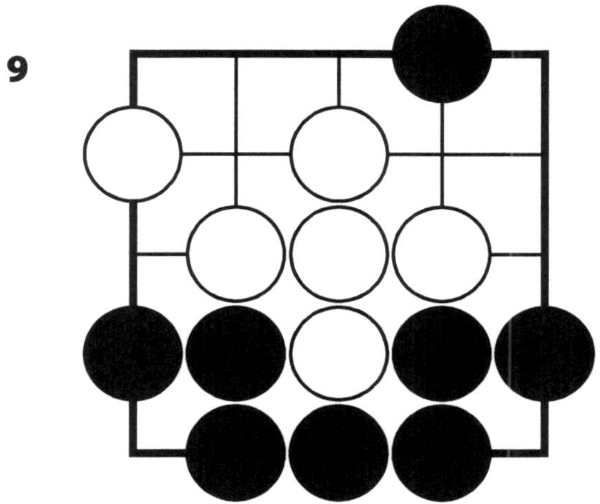

Black has two points...

10

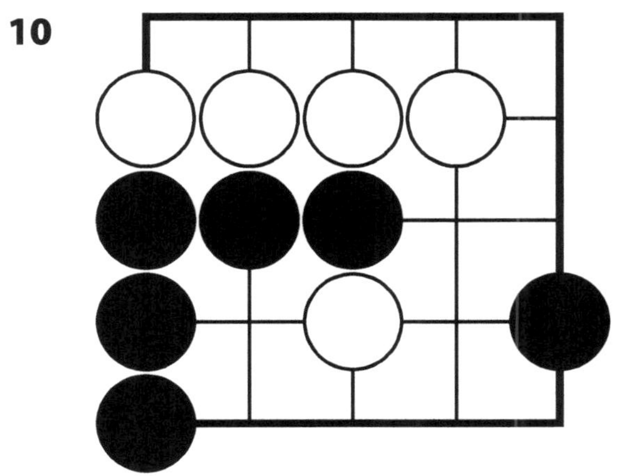

How to take care of...

Solution 9 **Black wins by one point.**

[1] [2] [3]

Dia. 1 (Correct) Black's placement at 1 and the kosumi 3 are an exquisite combination. When White separates at 4, Black takes the neutral point. The upper side is now a seki. In the end, White captures a stone and Black wins by one point.

Dia. 2 (Failure) If Black plays 1 first, White makes two eyes. Now each side has two points. This is jigo and thus a failure for Black.

Dia. 3 (Variation) If White blocks after Black 1, Black can create the seki with 3 and 5 again. Black wins.

Solution 10 **Black wins by one point.**

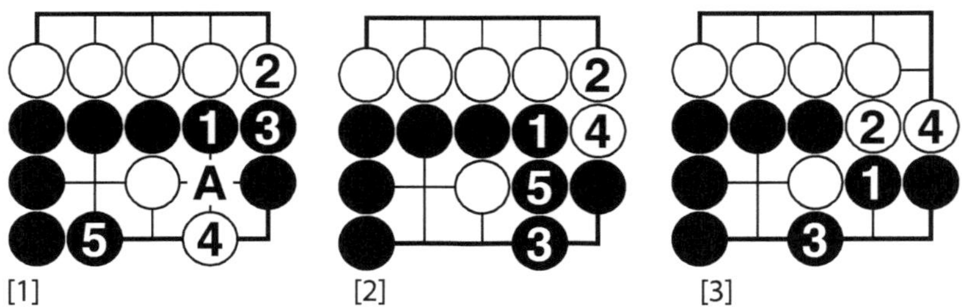

[1] [2] [3]

Dia. 1 (Failure) The only way to play is Black 1, but when White answers with 2, Black 3 is too greedy. White 4 creates a seki. Black loses by five points. If Black plays 3 at A, White 4 leads to the same result.

Dia. 2 (Correct) The correct answer is Black's hanging connection at 3. After White 4, Black connects at 5 and wins by one point.

Dia. 3 (Failure) Black 1 fails as White 2 and 4 finish the game with jigo.

11

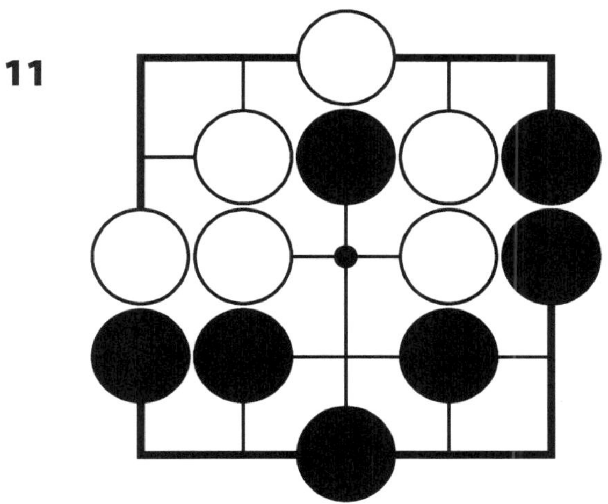

Abandoned and...

12

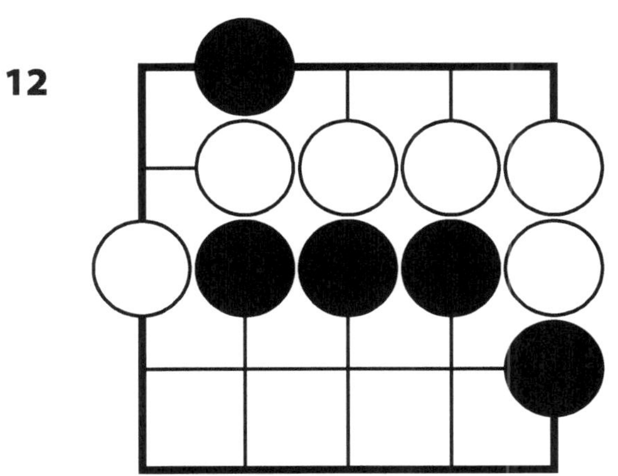

One move solves

Solution 11 **Black wins by one point.**

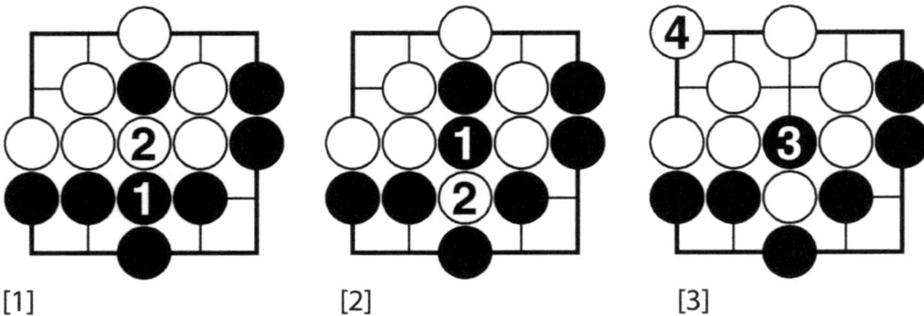

[1] [2] [3]

Dia. 1 (Failure) It seems Black 1 is the only choice to play, but this move fails. The game ends with White 2. Black loses by one point.

Dia. 2 (Correct) Black 1 is a clever move and let's White capture with 2...

Dia. 3 (Continuation) When Black takes back at 3, White has to create two eyes with 4. Now, Black wins by one point.

Solution 12 **Black wins by one point.**

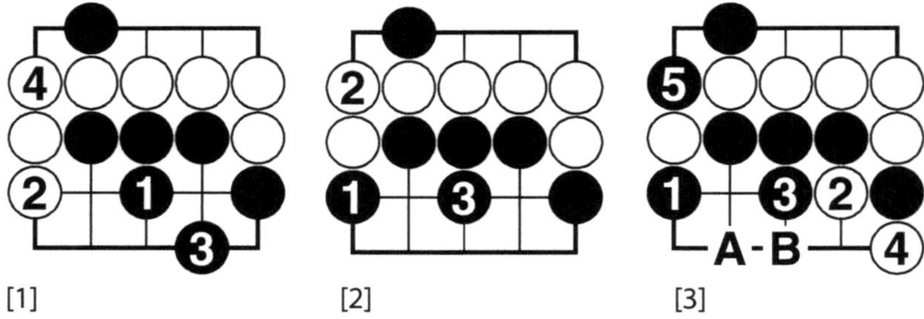

[1] [2] [3]

Dia. 1 (Failure) Defending the cut with 1 is not good enough. White pushes in at 2, and Black has to live with 3. Black is left with two points and loses by a total of four.

Dia. 2 (Correct) The correct answer is blocking at 1. After White 2, Black defends both cutting points with 3. Black wins by one point.

Dia. 3 (Variation) If White resists with the cut at 2, Black plays 3 and 5. Next, White might attack at A, but Black's counter at B would be sufficient. White cannot win this semeai.

13

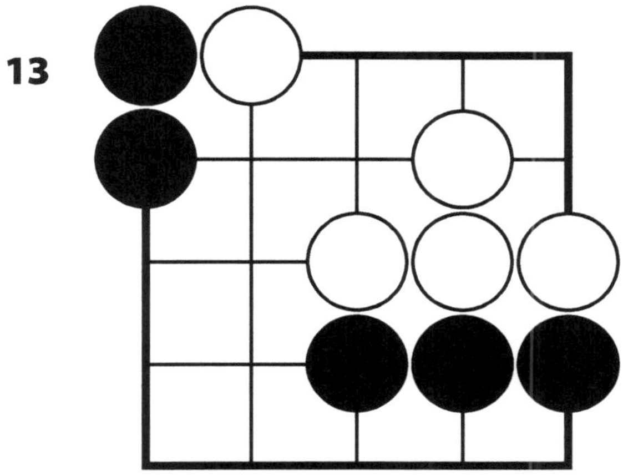

Two stones won't survive

14

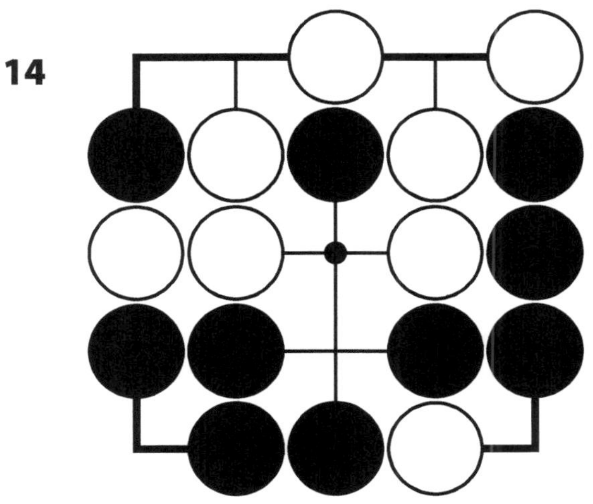

Order is important

Solution 13 Black wins by one point.

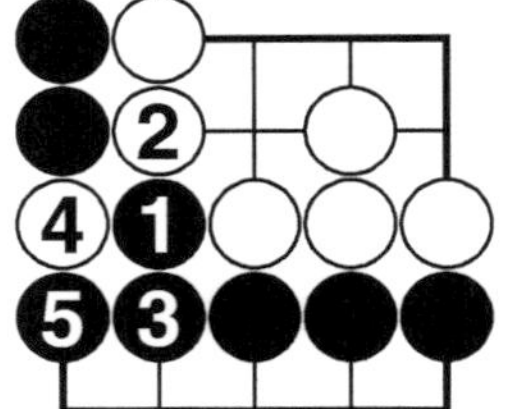

[1] *White 6 above 4*

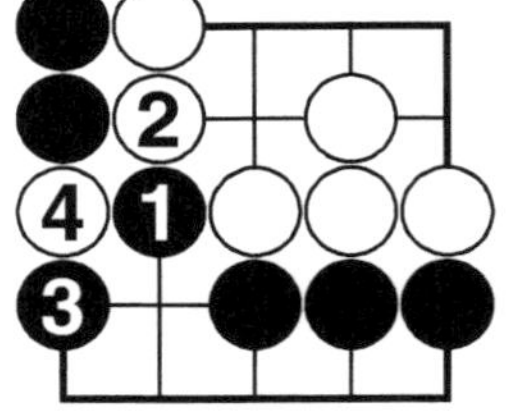

[2] *Black 5 above 4*

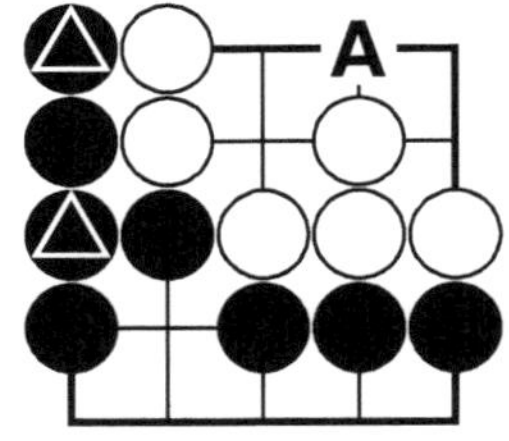

[3]

Dia. 1 (Failure) Black 1 is correct, but Black 3 is a mistake. The game ends with White 4 and White 6 connecting one line above 4. White has eight points in total and Black five. Black loses by three points.

Dia. 2 (Correct) There is no way to save Black's two stones in the corner, but they can still be used. A good move is Black 3 allowing Black to capture White 4 with 5. Black wins by one point.

Dia. 3 (Reference) In the end, when Black has played the marked stones to finish the game, White must play another move inside to defend against Black A.

Solution 14 Black wins by one point.

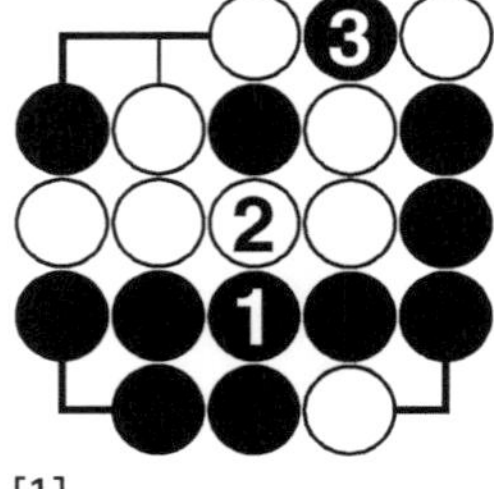

[1]

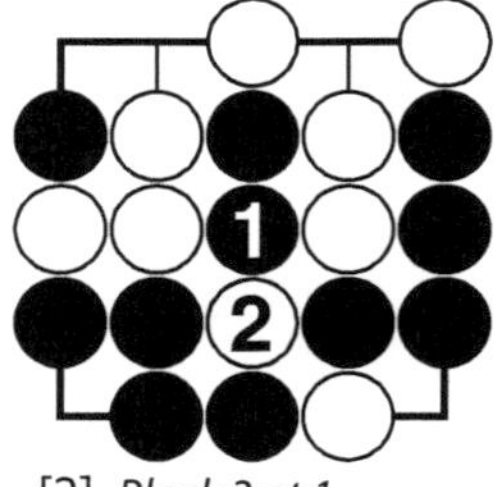

[2] *Black 3 at 1*

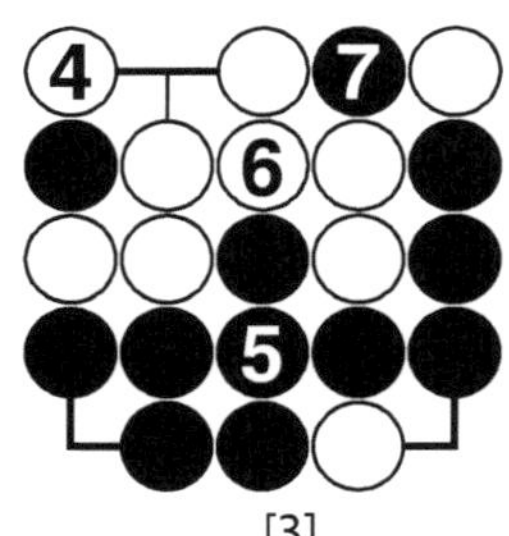

[3]

Dia. 1 (Failure) With 1 to 3, Black starts the ko. However, even if Black connects the ko, there will only be five points while White has six.

Dia. 2 (Correct) Black 1 is a good move. After White captures at 2, Black can retake a stone with 3 at 1.

Dia. 3 (Continuation) Next, White must make two eyes at 4. After Black connects at 5, White must protect the eye shape with 6. Black takes the ko with 7. This way, Black wins by one point.

15

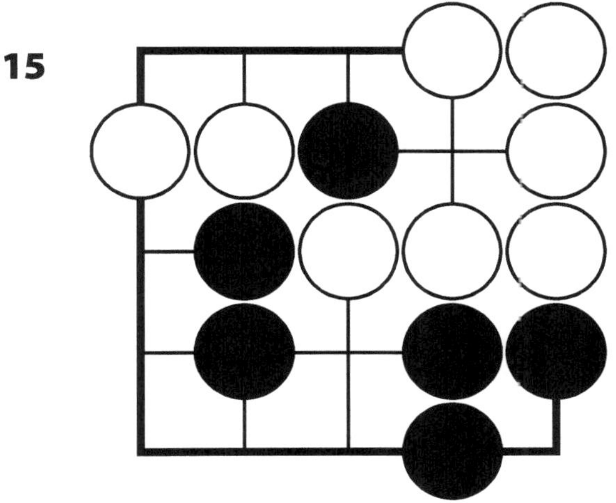

Gain the most out of a stone

16

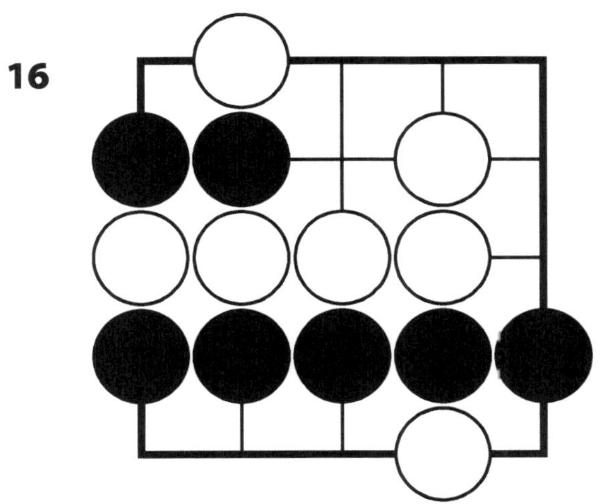

Two points of acute concern

Solution 15 Black wins by one point.

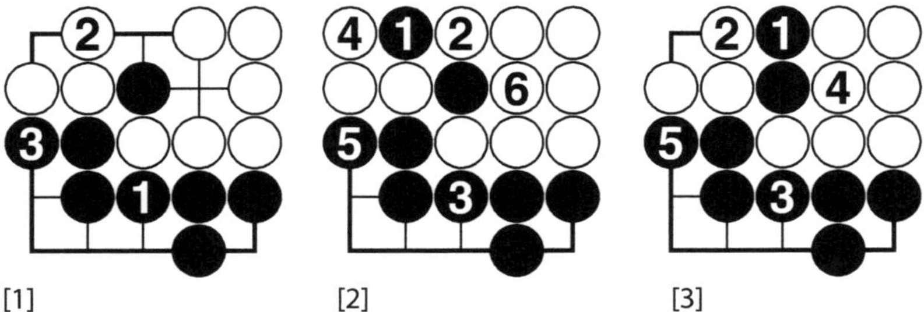

[1] [2] [3]

Dia. 1 (Failure) The game ends with Black 1 to 3. White 2 is a strong move. The result is jigo, a failure for Black.

Dia. 2 (Correct) Black 1 takes the vital point. White has no choice but to cut with 2. Black 3 and 5 force White to capture with 4 and 6. White's area has been reduced to four points. Black wins by one point.

Dia. 3 (Failure) Black's extension at 1 leads to the same result as in diagram 1. It's a failure.

Solution 16 Black wins by one point.

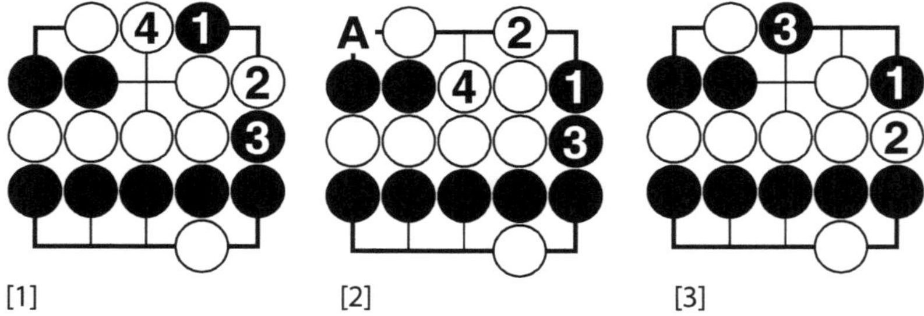

[1] [2] [3]

Dia. 1 (Failure) Black 1 is not a good move, but White 2 is. Black 3 is followed by White 4, and Black loses by three points. Black 1 at 3 would be answered by White with 2 as well.

Dia. 2 (Correct) Black's tesuji at 1 hits the vital point. The best thing to do for White is to draw back at 2. After Black 3, White must play 4 and later even at A. Black wins by one point.

Dia. 3 (Variation) If White answers with blocking at 2, Black creates a seki with 3.

17

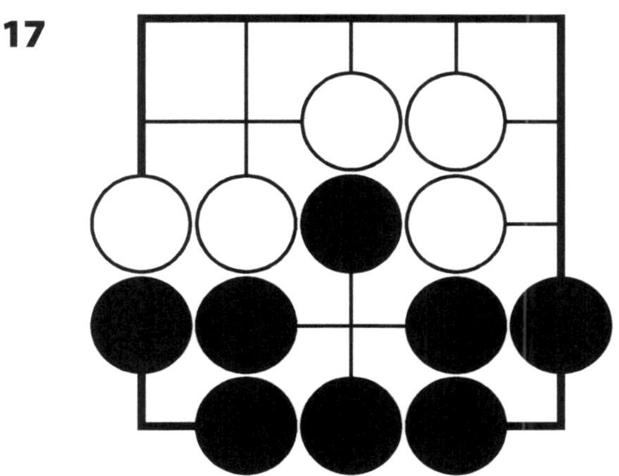

An obvious ko

18

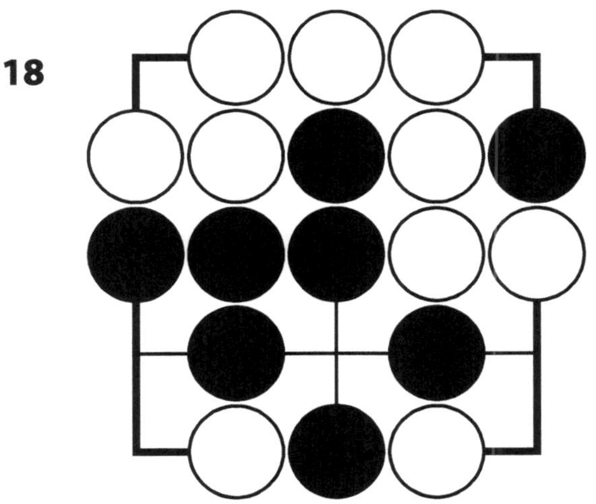

Where are the ko threats?

Solution 17 Black wins by one point.

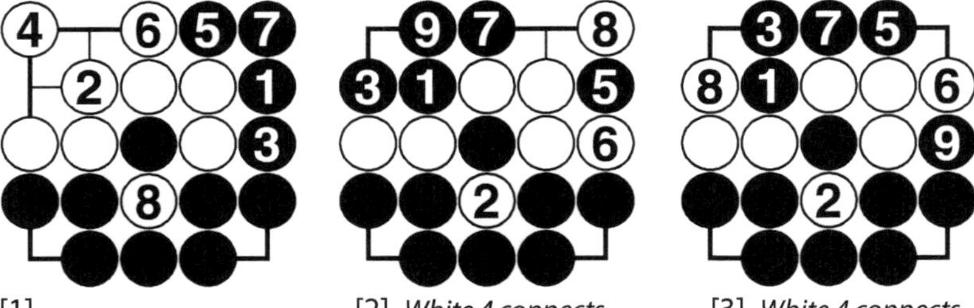

[1] [2] *White 4 connects* [3] *White 4 connects*

Dia. 1 (Failure) Black 1 is an endgame tesuji move, but White simply defends here at 2. Black connects at 3. Following the sequence up to White 8, it is White taking the ko first. White wins by one point.

Dia. 2 (Failure) It's good for Black to start with the cut at 1. However, after White 2, Black 3 is a failure. Even if Black continues with the moves 5 to 9, White has captured two stones in the end. So the result is jigo.

Dia. 3 (Correct) Black 3 is the correct answer, and Black 5 is another strong move. After Black 9, there is a seki at the top resulting in a one point win for Black.

Solution 18 Black wins by one point.

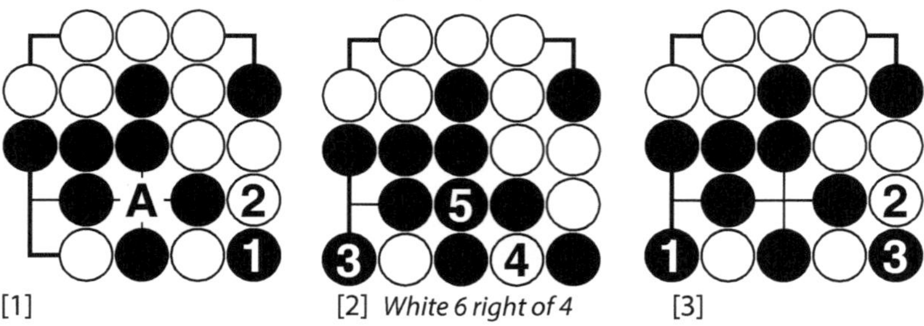

[1] [2] *White 6 right of 4* [3]

Dia. 1 (Failure) Black 1 is careless. This move doesn't work as White 2 reveals. Black is in atari, but cannot connect. If Black plays 1 at 2, White will capture at A. Black lacks a ko threat to fight the ko.

Dia. 2 (Continuation) Black has no choice but to capture a stone at 3. White takes the ko and Black again has no choice but to connect at 5. In the end, Black loses by one point.

Dia. 3 (Correct) Black 1 is a calm move solving the root of the problem. After White 2, Black takes the ko first and wins. The result is a one point win for Black.

19

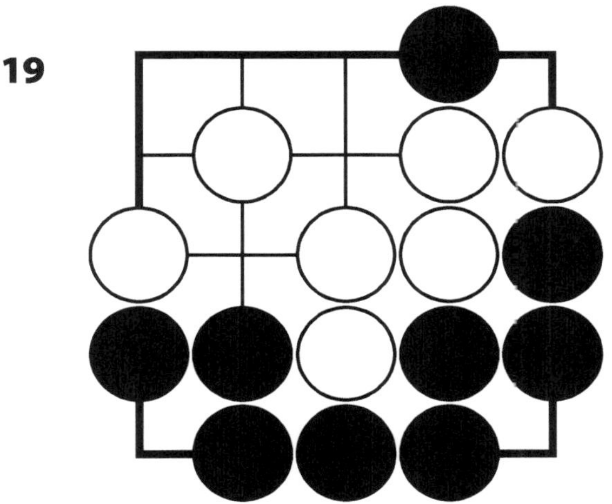

The key point

20

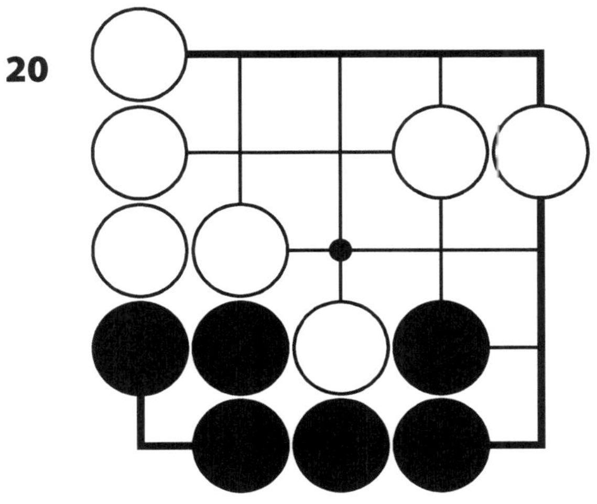

The usual way

Solution 19 Black wins by two points.

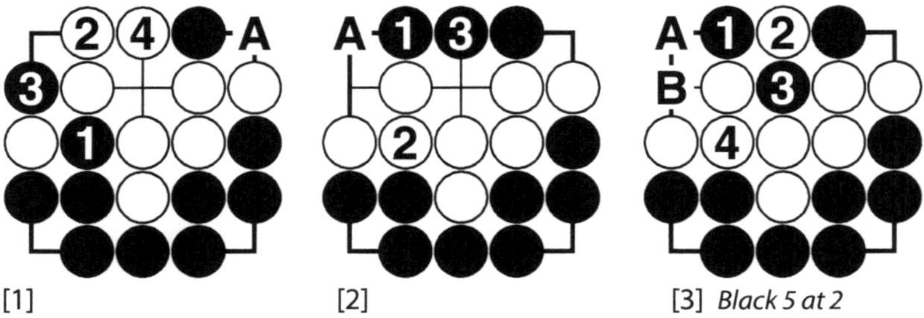

[1] [2] [3] *Black 5 at 2*

Dia. 1 (Failure) If Black plays 1, White simply responds at 2. After White 4, the game ends in jigo. White, of course, has to capture at A in the end.

Dia. 2 (Correct) Black 1 takes the key point and is the correct answer. After White 2, Black 3 is good enough. White cannot start a ko at A. The seki at the top ensures Black a win by two points.

Dia. 3 (Variation) There is only White 2, but after Black 3, White has to connect at 4. Black connects with 5 at 2, and White cannot start the ko at A. If White plays 4 at A, Black at 4, White at 2, and Black at B will follow. Again, White has no ko threat and is destroyed.

Solution 20 Black wins by two points.

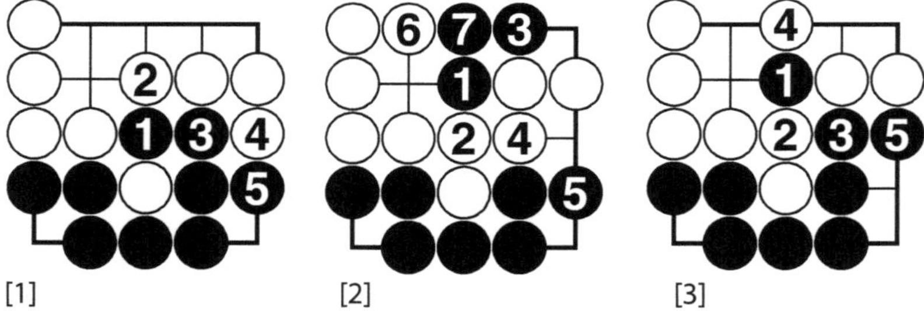

[1] [2] [3]

Dia. 1 (Failure) When Black captures a stone in the center, White blocks at 2. After Black 3 to 5, the game is over and White has gained one point more than Black.

Dia. 2 (Correct) The correct sequence is Black 1, White 2, and Black 3. After Black 7, White lives in seki, but Black has two eyes. Black wins by two points.

Dia. 3 (Variation) It is not good to cut with Black 3. This fails, as White now defends at 4. The game ends with Black 5, and a loss for Black.

21

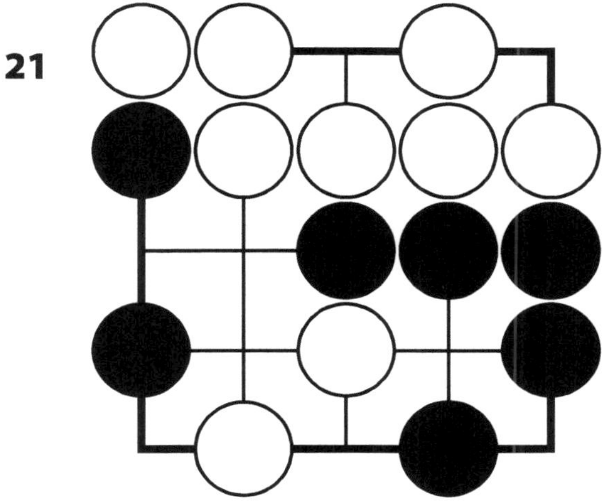

When one is greedy

22

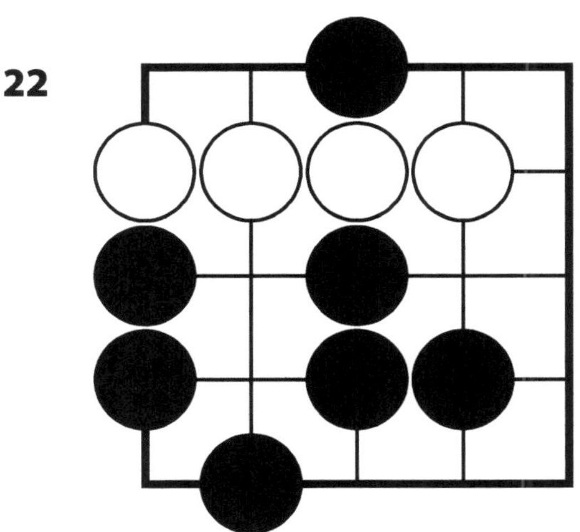

Step in!

Solution 21 Black wins by two points.

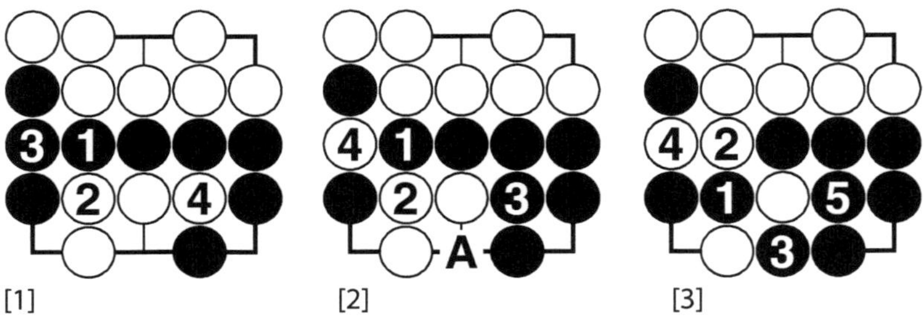

[1] [2] [3]

Dia. 1 (Failure) If Black is greedy and plays 1, White takes the vital point at 2. Black cannot win. Black 3 connects, and White 4 creates a seki. Losing by two points is a failure for Black.

Dia. 2 (Failure) If Black answers at 3, White captures at 4. Black has no ko threat and dies. It's the same result when Black plays 3 at A, White answers at 4.

Dia. 3 (Correct) Black 1 is the correct answer. There is not much choice but to play White 2 to Black 5. Black wins by two points.

Solution 22 Black wins by two points.

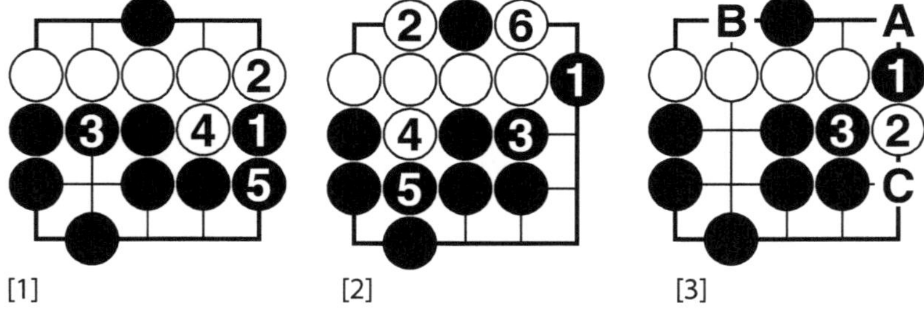

[1] [2] [3]

Dia. 1 (Failure) Black's kosumi at 1 and Black 3 are common sense, but this leads to a loss for Black. Black has to go a little further.

Dia. 2 (Correct) Black can advance to 1. White must defend at 2, and Black can continue with 3 to White 6. Black has five points, White only three. Black wins by two points.

Dia. 3 (Variation) If White counters with the hane at 2, Black plays 3 as well. If White now captures at A, Black kills White with a move at B. If White plays B, Black takes a stone at C. Either way, Black wins.

23

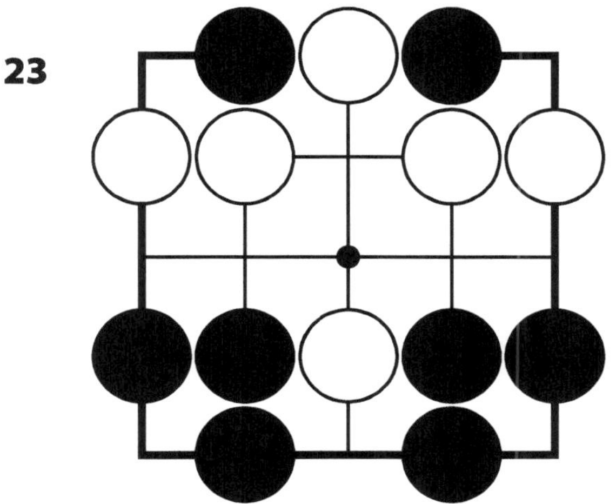

Symmetrical

24

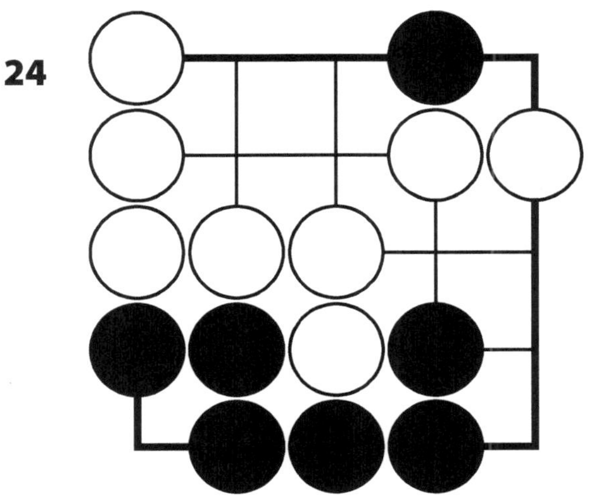

Inside or outside?

Solution 23 Black wins by one point.

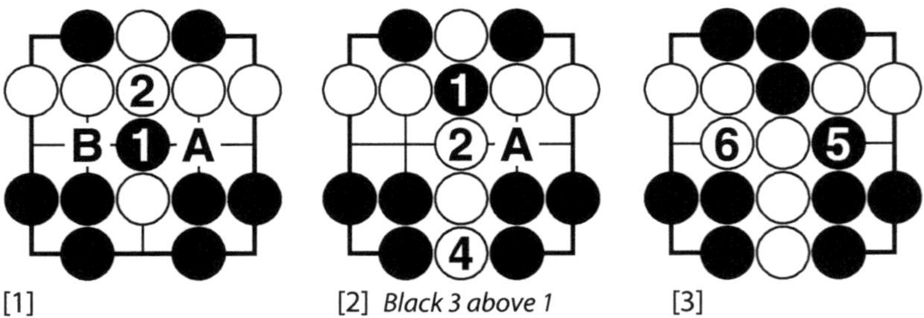

[1] [2] *Black 3 above 1* [3]

Dia. 1 (Failure) There seems no choice but to play in the center. White counters at 2. Next, White A and B are miai. Black has five points and White six. Black loses by one point.

Dia. 2 (Correct) Black advancing to 1 is a sharp move. White goes on top of it at 2. After Black connects, White separates Black's stones at the bottom. If White plays 4 at A instead, Black makes life at 4 while White would be dead.

Dia. 3 (Continuation) After Black cuts at 5 and White connects at 6, the whole board is seki. However, Black has captured one stone, so Black wins.

Solution 24 Black wins by two points.

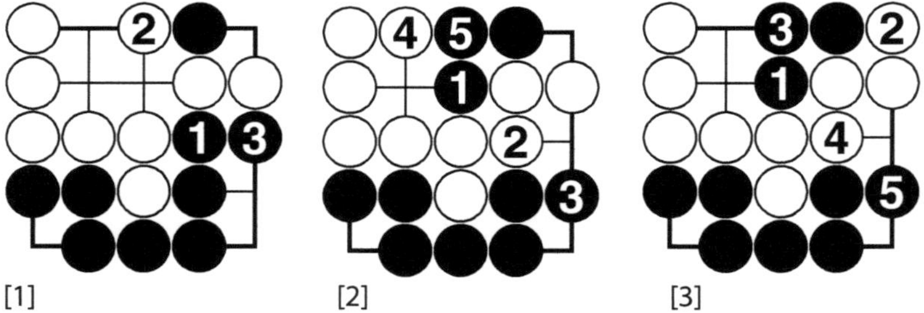

[1] [2] [3]

Dia. 1 (Failure) Black must not allow White to defend at 2. Black 1 and 3 are a failure. Black loses by three points.

Dia. 2 (Correct) Black 1 inside exploits the flaw in White's position. After White 2, Black makes life with 3. White has no choice but to create a seki with 4. The game ends with Black 5. There is no way for White to take away Black's eyes, so Black wins by two points.

Dia. 3 (Variation) White 2 is answered by Black's connection at 3. However, now White must protect at 4, so Black can make two eyes at 5.

25

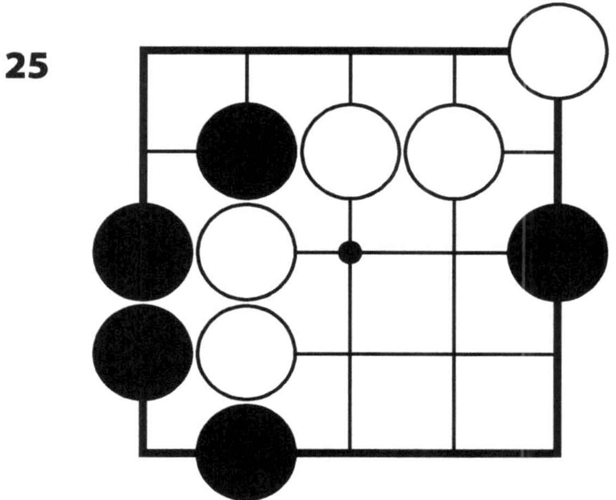

Even without eyes

26

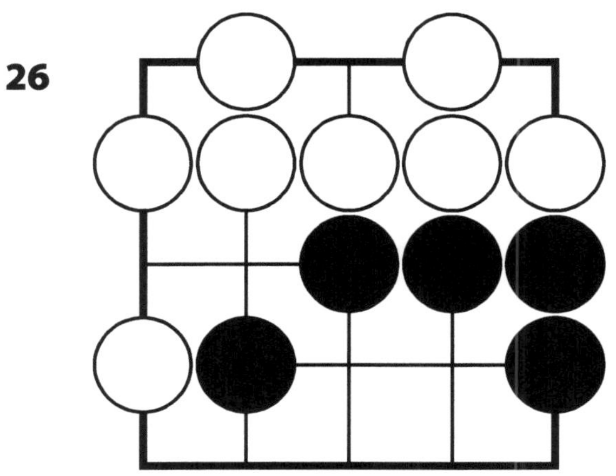

Bad tricks...

Solution 25 Black wins by one point.

[1]

[2] *White 6 at 1*

[3]

Dia. 1 (Failure) It is a failure for Black to play the atari at 1 and start a capturing race. White's throw-in at 4 is a strong counter. After White 6, Black cannot prevent being captured when White finally plays A.

Dia. 2 (Correct) The correct answer is Black's tesuji combination of 1 and 3. After Black 7, the whole board is seki. White has captured a stone, but Black wins by one point.

Dia. 3 (Reference) Black can connect at A and B to make an eye. If White prevents the eye by throwing in a stone, Black gains a point by capturing this stone. The same applies to the upper left corner.

Solution 26 Black wins by one point.

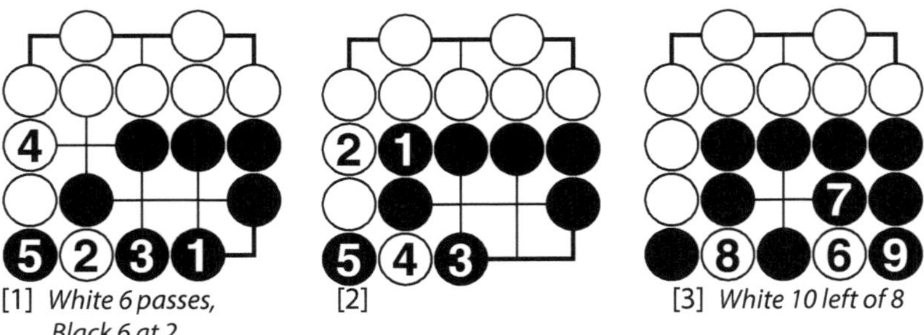

[1] *White 6 passes, Black 6 at 2*

[2]

[3] *White 10 left of 8*

Dia. 1 (Correct) It is correct to ensure eye shape with the kosumi at 1. Even if White attacks with 2, Black simply blocks at 3. After White 4, Black takes the ko first. There is no ko threat for White, so Black will connect and win by one point.

Dia. 2 (Failure) Black 1 and 3 are not good. After White 4, Black starts the ko with 5, but...

Dia. 3 (Continuation) ...this time White has a ko threat at 6. Black 7 to 9 are forced. White connects the ko and each side has four points. Jigo is a failure for Black.

27

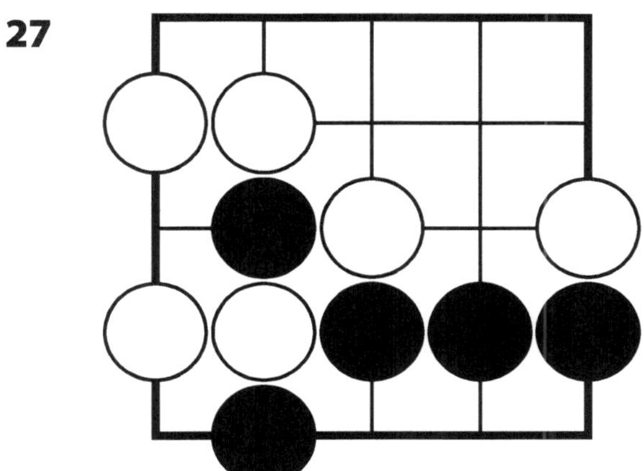

Even when divided

28

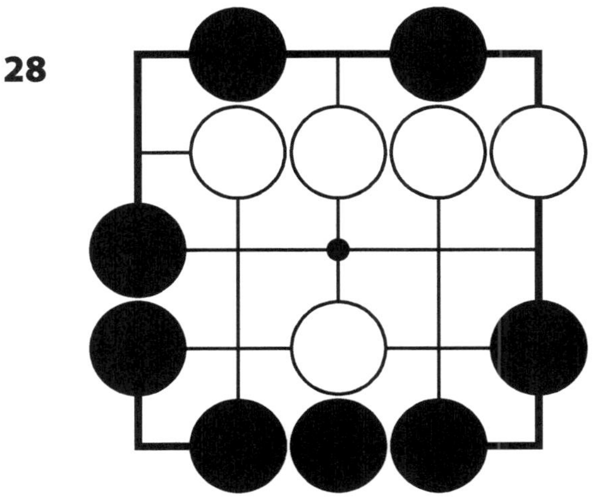

A big fight

Solution 27 **Black wins by one point.**

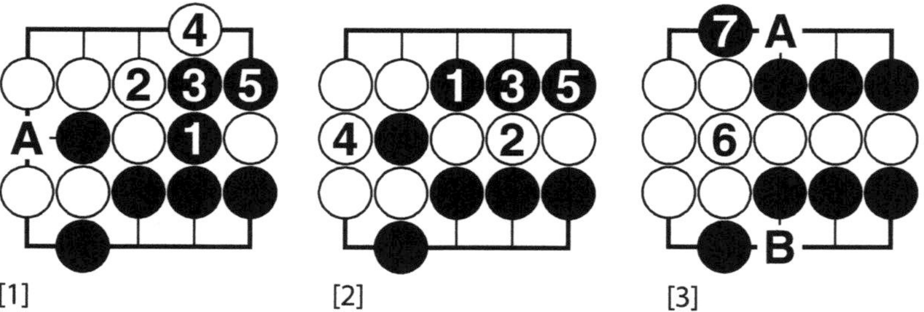

[1] [2] [3]

Dia. 1 (Failure) Black 1 and 3 are natural endgame moves, and Black 5 finishes the game. White has to capture at A. Each side has four points, a failure for Black.

Dia. 2 (Correct) Black 1 is playing a clever trick. After White 2, Black's squeeze with 3 and 5 is the correct follow up.

Dia. 3 (Continuation) White 6 connects, and Black continues at 7. There are two points, A and B: When Black connects here, White must throw in to prevent Black approaching. Black wins by the difference of the number of stones captured.

Solution 28 **Black wins by one point.**

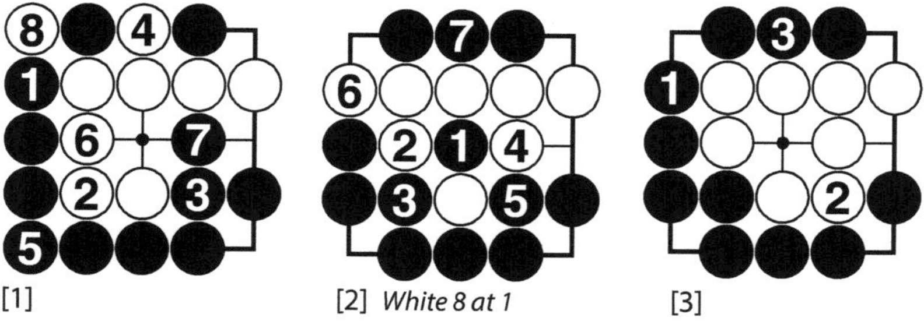

[1] [2] *White 8 at 1* [3]

Dia. 1 (Failure) Black 1 is a common move, but after White 2, Black cannot win. Even if Black makes an eye with 3, White can secure an eye with 4 as well. After Black 7, White starts the ko. While the whole board is seki, White has captured two stones. Black loses by two points.

Dia. 2 (Correct) Black 1 takes the key point. Black makes two eyes with 3 and 5, and then creates a seki at the top with 7. Black wins by one point.

Dia. 3 (Variation) If Black plays 1 instead of 5 in the previous diagram, White 2 and Black 3 lead to a whole board seki. There is one captured stone for White, so Black loses by one point.

29

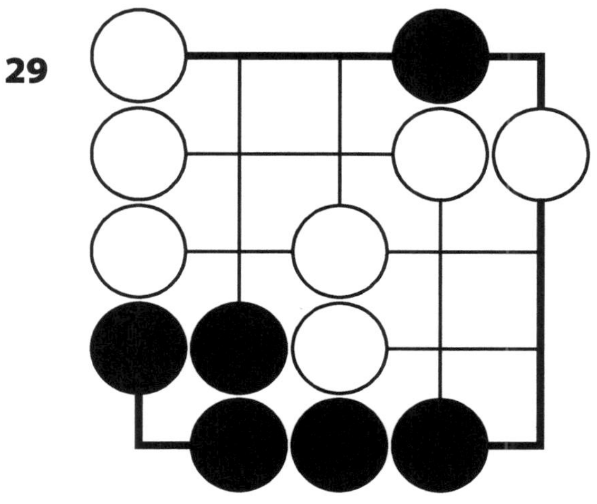

After the key point

30

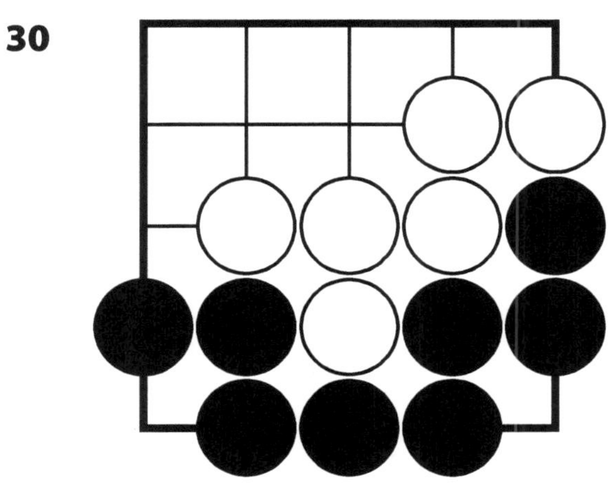

A change in the corner

Solution 29 Black wins by two points.

[1] [2] [3]

Dia. 1 (Failure) Starting with 1 and 3, Black can make life. White has to defend at 4. Black's territory after 5 and 7 is three points, but White has four points. Black loses by one point.

Dia. 2 (Variation) After White 2, Black can take White's eyes away. But after White 4 and Black 5, White counter attacks at 6. Black cannot win this semeai and dies.

Dia. 3 (Correct) It is a clever to attack with Black 1 from the inside. White resists with 2, and Black lives with 3 and 5. The best White can do is to create a seki up to 7. So Black wins by two points.

Solution 30 Black wins by two points.

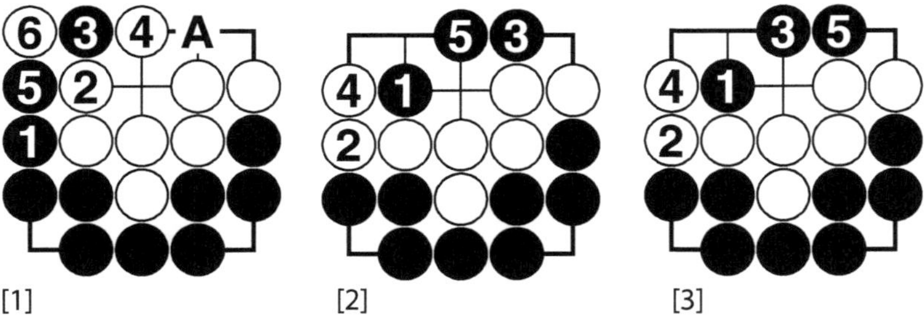

[1] [2] [3]

Dia. 1 (Failure) Black 1 is the normal move and is answered by White 2. Black cannot win. Even if Black tries 3, White 4 is a calm defense. After White 6, there is no ko threat for Black and White connects. Black loses by two points. The result is the same when Black plays 3 at 5 and White takes 3. White must not play 4 at 5, as Black has the strong counter at A.

Dia. 2 (Correct) Black 1 is the correct solution. White has no choice but to play 2. Now, Black creates a seki with 3 and 5.

Dia. 3 (Correct) Black can change the order of 3 and 5, which also works.

31

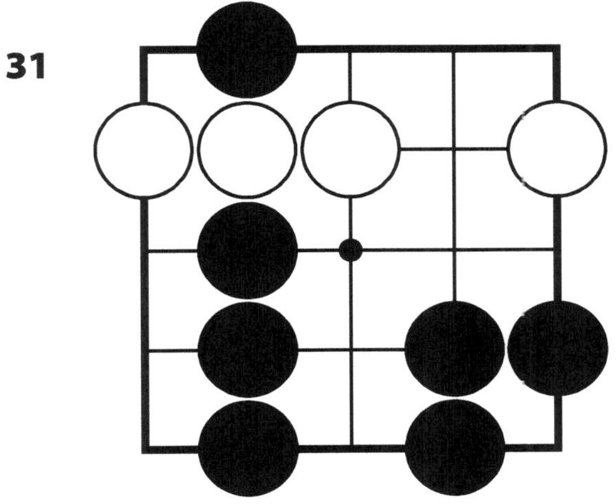

Black's iron wall

32

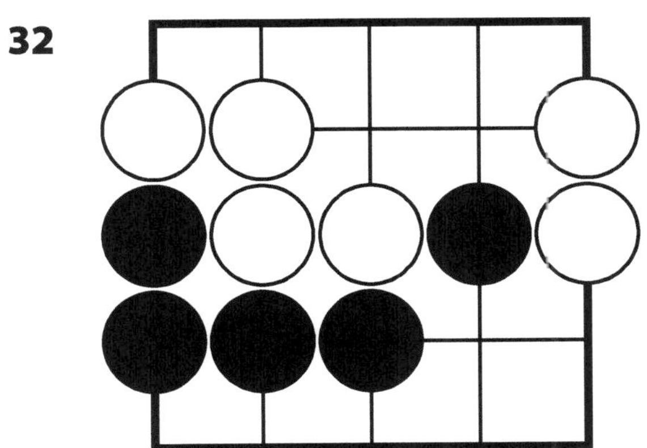

Advance or retreat

Solution 31 Black wins by three points.

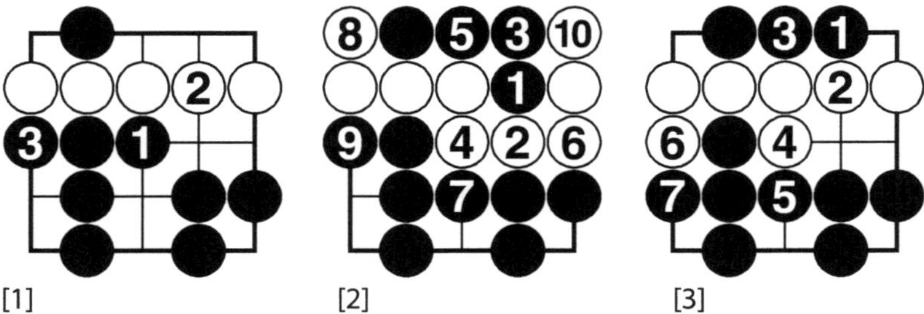

[1] [2] [3]

Dia. 1 (Failure) Blocking with 1 and 3 secures five points of territory for Black. But White encloses six points with 2. Black loses by one point. This is a failure.

Dia. 2 (Failure) Black's wedge at 1 is a good idea, but it is not successful because White responds with 2 and 4. After Black connects at 5, White captures four stones in the sequence up to White 10.

Dia. 3 (Correct) Black 1 is the correct answer. After White 2, Black creates a seki with 3. Black wins by three points. If White 2 at 3, Black simply extends to 2 and White cannot live.

Solution 32 Black wins by one point.

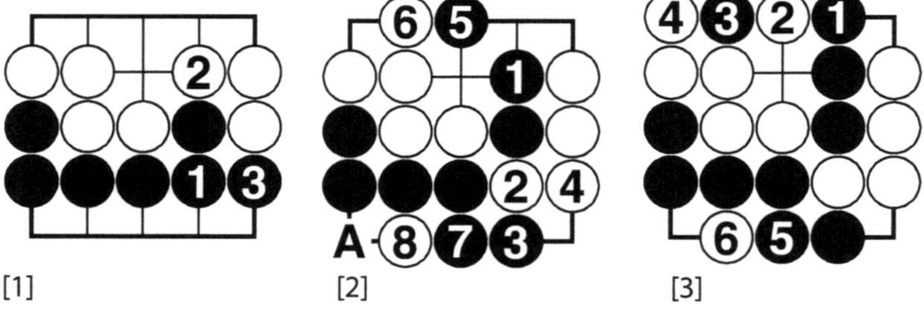

[1] [2] [3]

Dia. 1 (Failure) Black 1 and White 2 are ground solid moves. After Black 3, White has six points and Black only five. Black loses by one point.

Dia. 2 (Correct) Pushing forward with Black 1 is correct. After White cuts, Black plays the atari 3 and then takes the crucial point at 5. White 6 creates a whole board seki. But after Black 7, White needs to throw in at 8. Black captures this stone at A and wins by one point.

Dia. 3 (Variation) Black 1 instead of 5 in the previous diagram is a failure. After White 2, Black's throw-in at 3 is needed to maintain the seki. The result is jigo, a failure for Black.

33

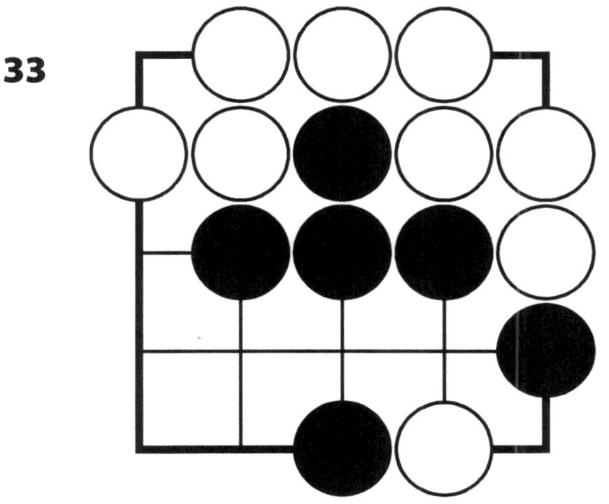

Steady is best

34

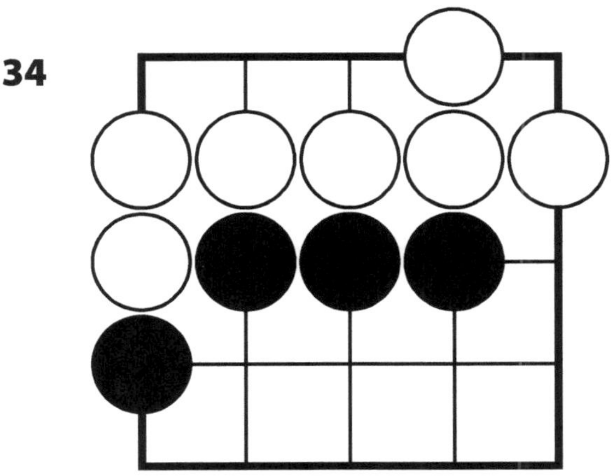

Be sure to get it right

Solution 33 Black wins by five points.

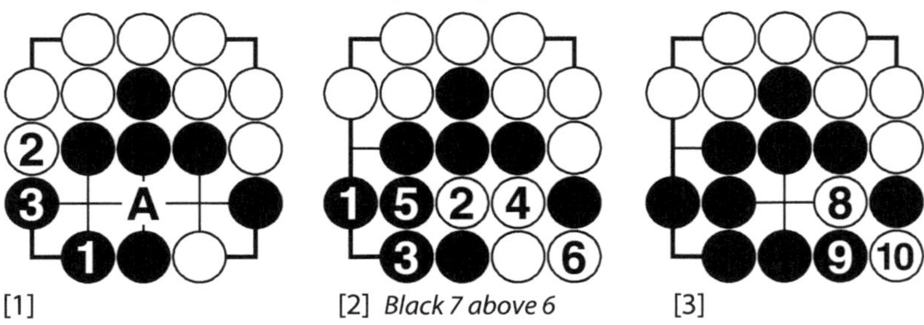

[1] [2] *Black 7 above 6* [3]

Dia. 1 (Correct) Black 1 on the first line is the correct answer. After White 2 and Black 3, Black wins by five points. Black 1 at 2 is a failure, as White will counter at A and create a seki. This would clearly be a loss for Black.

Dia. 2 (Failure) Black 1 is a poor attempt, as White answers at 2. This leads to an "under the stones" sequence where Black 7 captures four stones.

Dia. 3 (Continuation) The game continues with White 8 and 10 starting a ko. Black has no chance to win this ko due to the lack of a ko threat.

Solution 34 Black wins by three points.

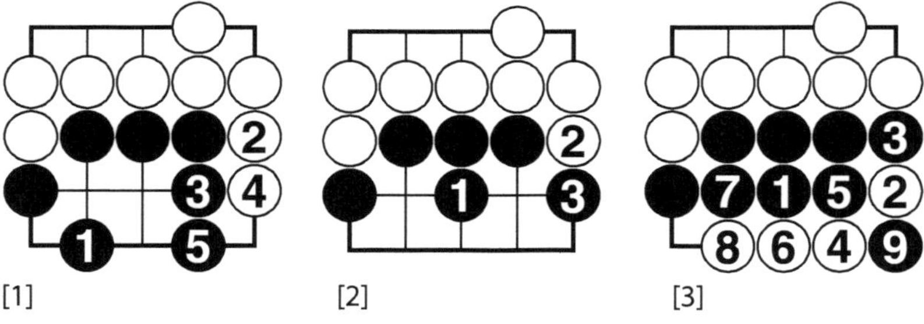

[1] [2] [3]

Dia. 1 (Failure) Black's hanging connection is a standard defense, but now White rushes in with 2 and 4. After Black 5, each side has four points. Jigo is a failure for Black.

Dia. 2 (Correct) Black 1 is a good move, defending both the left and the right side. After White 2, Black can block at 3 and wins by three points.

Dia. 3 (Variation) If White jumps in at 2 and continues at 4, Black can defend with 5. Up to Black 9, there is a ko which Black takes first. Black must not play 5 at 6, as White will answer at 8 and create a seki at the bottom. Black would lose in this case.

35

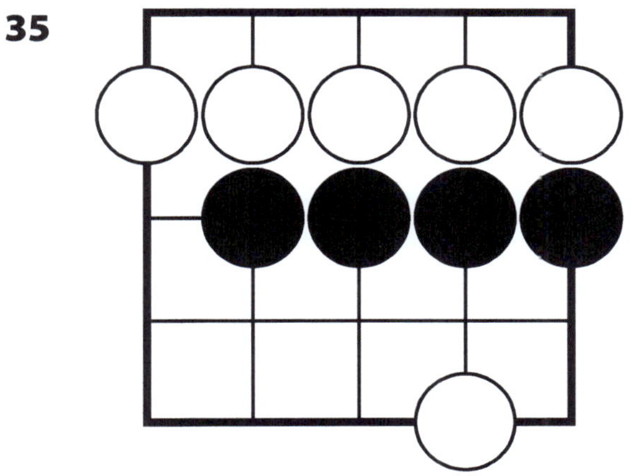

Not too big

36

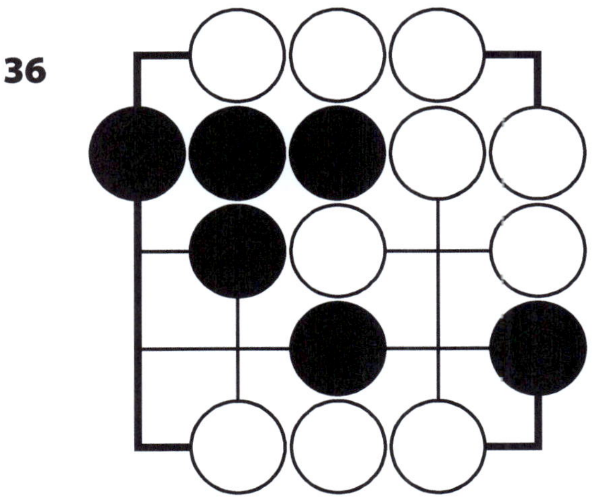

Strange shape

Solution 35 Black wins by four points.

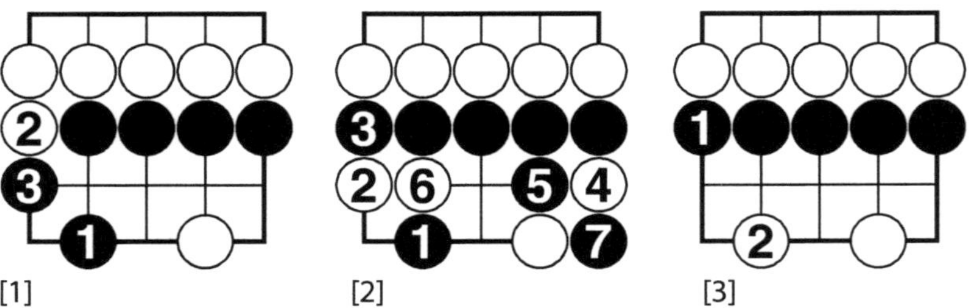

[1] [2] [3]

Dia. 1 (Correct) White's stone still has some aji, so Black must defend against it. Black 1 takes the critical point, and the game ends with White 2 and Black 3. Black wins by four points.

Dia. 2 (Variation) If White counters with 2, Black separates at 3. Next, White 4 is answered by Black 5. After White 6 and Black 7, there is a ko, but White lacks a ko threat. So Black wins.

Dia. 3 (Failure) Black 1 is not a proper defense. After White 2, White's stones cannot be captured, and Black loses.

Solution 36 Black wins by one point.

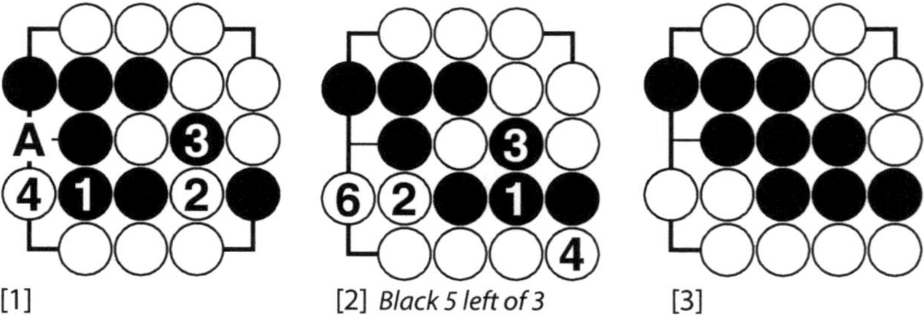

[1] [2] *Black 5 left of 3* [3]

Dia. 1 (Failure) After Black 1, White separates at 2. Black captures at 3, and White takes another liberty from Black. Next, if Black approaches at A, White takes the ko to the left of 3. There is no way for Black to win. Black 1 at 3 at doesn't work either. White plays 2 again, and Black loses.

Dia. 2 (Correct) Black 1 and 3 are the correct solution. White 4 creates a seki. Since there is one captured stone, Black wins by one point.

Dia. 3 (Reference) The final position from the previous diagram is shown again. Each of White's groups has a single eye, while Black's group has no eye at all – a strange shape.

BLACK TO PLAY

TRAIN THE BASICS OF GO

This book series accompanies the go player from his first steps until reaching shodan, the first master rank.

A wide range of problems covering all fundamental topics is laid out across six books to meet the needs of any growing player.

5 KYU – 1 KYU

10 KYU – 5 KYU

15 KYU – 10 KYU

20 KYU – 15 KYU

25 KYU – 20 KYU

30 KYU – 25 KYU

BOARD N'STONES

How to Play Go the AI way! by Yamada Shinji 6p

The AI style may seem confusing because there are so many tactics far away from traditional thinking. The study of the new techniques introduced by AI has lead to their rapid spread and adoption. Today they are applied by pros almost as a matter of course. This book summarizes the findings from the study of AI techniques and explains them in illustrative diagrams.

Aji's Quest by Colette Bezio

Enthusiastic, cheeky, a little impatient, but certainly not hindered by any prior knowledge, Aji allows himself to be sent by Master Tenuki on a quest to the top of mountain Moyo. After all, he wants to become 27th Dan as soon as possible. Along the way, he experiences bizarre adventures...

How Strong is Your Go?

This book is both test and training. It will not only help you to assess your skill level, but also to identify your strengths and weaknesses in the game of Go. In a total of eight chapters, you are asked to solve the exercises within a given time limit. With the help of the evaluation tables you will be able to determine where you are roughly located within the kyu and dan ranks.

The Elephant in the Paddy. Tsumego in Pictures by Izumi Hase

In this book you will experience Go problems from a very different angle. The creative and amusing pictures composed of black and white stones involve amazing life-and-death exercises.